HEAVENLY SPRINGS

HEAVENLY SPRINGS

Portions for the Sabbaths of a year, selected from the diary, letters and sermons of Andrew A. Bonar, D.D. by his daughter

MARJORY BONAR

*

"Sabbath-days are well-days in the desert journey, days when we fill the waterskins, to journey on to another well."

ANDREW A. BONAR

THE BANNER OF TRUTH TRUST

THE BANNER OF TRUTH TRUST
3 Murrayfield Road, Edinburgh, EH12 6EL
PO Box 621, Carlisle, Pennsylvania 17013, USA

*

First published 1904
First Banner of Truth edition 1986

*

ISBN 0 85151 479 0

*

Printed and bound in Great Britain by
Hazell Watson & Viney Limited,
Member of the BPCC Group,
Aylesbury, Bucks

CONTENTS

CONTENTS

"Is the wilderness before thee—
    Desert lands where drought abides?
Heavenly springs shall there restore thee,
    Fresh from God's exhaustless tides.

Though thy way be long and dreary,
    Eagle strength He'll still renew:
Garments fresh and feet unweary
    Tell how God hath brought thee through."

" Good Shepherd, gratify Thyself
by saving me ! "

" I have gone astray like
a lost sheep; seek Thy
servant."

PSALM cxix. 176.

I

THE WAY OF SALVATION

FOR about two weeks past, ever since I read a passage in Guthrie's *Saving Interest*, I have had a secret, joyful hope that I really have believed on the Lord Jesus. If now at length I have reached a place of safety, it is solely through Divine grace. I did nothing but receive.

"It is to show the 'exceeding riches of His grace' that the Lord gives a whole eternity of blessedness to the man who, like the dying thief, has only been leaning on Him for a few hours."

"Divine grace pays everything, and gives us the benefit of all."

"We are asked to accept this salvation, to let this love into our heart, without shedding a tear, except it be a tear of love and gratitude."

"Unbelief is just pushing away the hand that comes to offer us gifts."

"A hearty receiver of God's gifts is welcome above all others to His presence."

"As many as receive Christ, God receives them."

2

" The Lord is so anxious to bless you that He will reward you for believing on Him. He will reward you for having confidence in Him. He will reward you for coming to drink of the living water."

" ' *He giveth grace to the humble*,' to those who do not come with a price in their hand, who simply expect it as a gift. '*He giveth grace to the lowly*,' who give *Him* nothing, who bring their empty vessels and say, ' Lord, fill them ! ' "

" The work of Christ is the open door for the sinner, but Christ Himself stands behind, waiting to welcome him."

" ' *Justified by faith* ' is the way we get hold of Him. ' *By His grace* ' is the way He gets hold of us."

" O men and brethren, look at that Cross and listen to what it says : ' *He that hath the Son hath life.* ' I often think when the Lord is thus pressing you to accept Christ, that He has not only stood at the door and knocked, but He has, as it were, opened the door a little to try to persuade you ! "

" If Cæsar's penny has Cæsar's image and superscription, this Ransom-money has the stamp of Godhead, and that is ' *freely.* ' "

" A child does not ask, ' How am I to take the gift ? ' but, 'Is it for *me* ? ' "

" He has pardon for you ; and the moment

you touch that pierced Hand and say,
'I have come for the payment,' you get
forgiveness."

"One day is enough for any man's salvation."

" O let the river of life rise higher
in my soul."

" They go from strength
to strength."

PSALM lxxxiv. 7.

May 16, 1848.

"ONE hour might make Jericho fall were faith in its mountain-removing exercise."

August 15, 1852.

Thinking of the few that seem to advance in grace, was cheered by this, that touching even the hem of His garment is salvation.

May 16, 1863.

I see more reason to be humble before other believers, however far behind they may sometimes seem, for that one spark of faith may be kindled into a bright flame any moment, and then with Christ for the fuel of the fire, O how these souls that seem now so low and feeble will burn and shine in the kingdom of God !

"Christ is not censorious. He comes to see if He can find just a grain of faith in your heart, and that pleases Him well."

"There was a defect in the faith of many

who came to Christ to be healed. But it was not the strength of their faith Christ looked to, but the reality of it; and they got the cure, though the hand that touched Him trembled."

"How strange it is that there is such a slowness in our souls to trust, and, even after we have begun, to believe all."

"Faith dwells at Jerusalem. Full assurance goes into the palace and sees the king's face."

"Faith renders the purest worship to God that can be offered."

"'*I will give him the morning-star.*' The fulfilment of that old word, 'He *will beautify the meek with salvation.*'"

"The Lord does not wish the sinner to get safety only. He wishes him to get into a paradise of joy and peace."

"The Spirit of liberty delivers us from the bondage of mere religion. He not only does this in a certain measure, but in a very full measure. He brings us into a large place. You are not to think He takes us out of the deep waters and makes us stand shivering on the shore."

"Why are Gideon and Barak spoken of for their faith—Barak who said, 'If Deborah does not go with me I will not go'—and Gideon who said, 'How shall I save Israel?'

Their faith gained strength as they went at the Lord's bidding."

"The Jews have a tradition that some of the mariners went with Jonah to Nineveh. They did not know what one man can do with whom God is."

"Faith always has wages paid by Him to whom faith looks up."

" Thy people are no longer heavy-laden with sins, but they are heavy-laden with benefits."

"My cup runneth over."
PSALM xxiii. 5.

9

THANKFULNESS

October 21, 1850.

I SEE that, rightly understood, it is as solemn a thing to be crowned with mercies as to be crushed with affliction.

December 10, 1861.

Last night I dreamed that I got such a view of God's kindness and benefits to me, that for some time my throat felt choked. I could find no way of giving utterance to my overwhelming feeling of wonder. When I awoke the savour of this still remained with me.

"You will notice that you far oftener meet a man labouring under a sense of sin than one labouring under a sense of mercies. We pick out all the little crosses and troubles of our life and mourn over them, and forget our mercies. The whole burden of our life is mercy, mercy, mercy."

THIRD SUNDAY

" We should be always wearing the garment of praise, not just waving a palm now and then ! "

" Thanksgiving is the very air of heaven." " When we have real confidence in exercise it will manifest itself either in prayer or in song, oftenest perhaps in prayer. In heaven it manifests itself in song."

" Pharaoh forgot all God's judgments. Do not we forget almost all His mercies ? "

" No fear of our suffering from too much of an overflowing cup if *He* fills it, and we take it from His hand, looking all the while in His face. He knows best what to give. ' *Your heavenly Father knoweth* ' has a store of comfort in it."

" There are some saints who weep so much over their imperfect holiness that they never rejoice."

" All we get is not got by praying. We often get a great deal we never ask for. There are some blessings that are altogether His giving."

" Many a temptation has been baffled,

many a difficulty faced successfully, and many a sorrow calmed by a song of praise."

"I do not think we ever pray the Lord's Prayer with all our heart without laying up something we shall be thankful for in the future."

" Let us seek to be delivered from trifling prayers, and contentment with trifling answers."

" When they had prayed, the place was shaken."

ACTS iv. 31.

ALL-PRAYER

September 4, 1842.

I WAS living very grossly, namely, labouring night and day in visiting, with very little prayerfulness. I did not see that prayer should be the main business of every day.

February, 1846.

" O brother, pray ; in spite of Satan, pray ; spend hours in prayer ; rather neglect friends than not pray ; rather fast, and lose breakfast, dinner, tea, and supper—and sleep too—than not pray. And we must not talk about prayer, we must pray in right earnest. The Lord is near. He comes softly while the virgins slumber. You may almost hear the breathing of the slumberers, and the tread of Him who comes into the camp as David did to Saul's, ere ever we are aware."

November 8, 1853.

Prayer, prayer, prayer, must be more a business than it has been.

" Prayer is seed sown on the heart of God."

"God likes to see His people shut up to this, that there is no hope but in prayer. Herein lies the Church's power against the world."

"Fasting is abstaining from all that interferes with prayer."

"It is a sign that the blessing is not at hand when God's people are not praying much."

"When we ask a little the Lord is slow to give it us. When we ask great things He hastens to give us them."

"Delayed answers may be very abundant answers."

"Ask God for anything, but let Him judge as to the manner and measure of the giving."

"Every time God hears us cry 'Abba, Father,' He remembers Christ's prayer in Gethsemane."

"I don't wonder that Peter says we ought to have more grace than we have. 'Add to your faith virtue,' &c. Suppose one of Jacob's sons had come back from Egypt with only a small sackful of corn and his father says to him, 'Is that all you have got?' 'Yes, all.' 'Had he no more to give? Did he grudge it?' 'No, but that was all I asked for.' Another of Jacob's sons comes with full sacks of corn. He needs six asses to carry them.

, How did you get them all?' 'Just as my brother here got his little sackful. *I asked for them.'*"

"When any passage of Scripture is brought home to us it is equivalent to God coming to us and saying '*Ask what I shall give thee.*' The apostle says, 'Ask of Him who giveth liberally and upbraideth not.' God might well reproach us with our carelessness, with not trading with our talent. He will not upbraid. Perhaps we put away some blessing last year, we thought it was too great. It is great things we expect from a liberal God. When the dying thief said, '*Lord, remember me when Thou comest into Thy kingdom,*' Christ said, 'Not only when I come into My kingdom, but to-day thou shalt be with Me.'"

" If Thy people cannot say they
have come to the land where
they hunger no more, neither
thirst any more, they can at
least say they neither hunger
nor thirst while the Lamb
is leading them through the
desert."

" He that hath mercy on
them shall lead them."

ISA. xlix. 10.

THROUGH THE DESERT

February 7, 1865.

" OUR house is not what it was, but the Lord is the same. O that I may be able to use Him as the true and only Lethe, in drinking of which I shall forget what I have lost."

August 24, 1867.

To-day I was thinking on Gen. xli. 51, 52, noticing that God's Lethe was in some degree fruitfulness in the time of affliction.

" God is saying to me ' *You have dwelt at this mountain long enough,*' and He is also saying ' Arise, journey onwards to the Promised Land.' Driven out of a rest here that was ready to ensnare the soul and make it self-indulgent, He cries, ' Be done with this for ever, and go on to a better.' And I am struck with noticing that He makes so little account of the wilderness that lies between. He puts the rest out of which He shakes us, side by side with the rest of the kingdom."

FIFTH SUNDAY

"God knows best how to ripen a soul for His own presence in glory."

"Trials are the opening of channels for more grace."

"Our Maker fashions our lot as well as fashions our frames."

"There is nothing in your lot takes Him by surprise, though it takes you by surprise."

"The Lord chooses our lot for us here, and He chooses our mansion for us above."

"It is pleasant work Christ gives us to do for Him, and it is vineyard work. There are clusters of grapes to refresh us, there is the shade of the vines, and there are songs to cheer the heart, and visits of the Master."

"It is only rebels who dwell in a dry land."

"God will not have an unlet house in New Jerusalem, no mansion where the grass grows before the door. Each mansion is reserved for some one. Our inheritance is reserved in heaven for us."

"*The Lord went before them by aay in a pillar of a cloud, to lead them the way*" (Ex. xiii. 21). Their past experience was not of great use to the Israelites in their journeyings. They needed always to consult God. If you think you will get through anything because you got through before, you will certainly fail You must ask fresh counsel of God an.

consult with Him continually ; and since the
pillar-cloud and not your own experience
is your guide, see that you make it so.   Perhaps some Israelite, looking on the burning
sands all around and thinking of the scorching
heat, would say, ' What if this continue ?
What if that friend should die ?   What if the
little ones be worn out ? '   Let us follow the
pillar-cloud and not trouble ourselves with
' ifs.' "

" Oh to be as Enoch till I die ! "

" Let us draw near."
HEB. X. 22.

COMMUNION WITH GOD

February 6, 1843.

HAVE been struck at noticing how often, especially no later than yesterday, in going forth to preach, I was like one seeking his own entrance into the holy place and fellowship with God ; not like one coming out from enjoying communion to speak to others.

July 21, 1843.

I see plainly that fellowship with God is not means to an end, but is to be the end itself. I am not to use it as a preparation for study or for Sabbath labour, but as my chiefest end, the likest thing to heaven.

"I have just been thinking over that promise to Israel, ' *Their soul shall be as a watered garden, and they shall sorrow no more at all.*' What a day ! Every plant of grace growing in the glorious Sun, watered by the Holy Spirit ; no serpent in the bowers of that garden ; no sorrow, because nothing to vex the heavenly Husbandman. I am sure my soul is no more like this than Eden was like the wilderness of Judah. I think my soul is like some of the vine-terraces on the hills of Palestine—the vine-dresser needs to bring soil, and then to build it up lest the very rains sent to bless it should sweep it out of its place. Constant care and training is the only process to keep it a vineyard at all. 'Grace' is a sweeter sound every day."

July 25, 1869.

I see that I will need every day more and more in the morning, before any business begins, a cup of the new wine of the kingdom —fellowship with God.

"God never withdraws from fellowship with us. It is we who withdraw from fellowship with Him. Often we have looked at the waves and listened to the winds, when we might have been walking with Christ on the waters."

"Dwell in the tabernacle under the shadow of the Almighty, and not a drop of wrath shall fall on a hair of your head. Walk, too, in the light of the cloud of glory over the mercy-seat. It is New Jerusalem glory."

"If you do not labour fervently in prayer that you may be '*perfect and complete in all the will of God*,' you will be dwarfed Christians.

You will be like one standing at the foot of Jacob's ladder, but never mounting up."

"You need hourly fellowship with Christ, and to have this you must be watchful. '*If ye abide in Me*,' that is faith. '*And My words abide in you*,' that is fellowship."

"Fellowship with God is very much the same thing as assurance."

"A single sin clinging to you will make you stand still in your progress."

"Take care of small sins, for if you get victory over small sins you have got pretty well on."

"What is a perfection in God should be a quality in us."

"You do not owe your steadfastness and consistency to anything in yourself. You owe it wholly to the unction of the Spirit within you."

"The fulness of the Spirit does not manifest itself in mere feeling. It always shows itself in some grace."

"The more you have of the wisdom and knowledge of God, the more you will attend to duty."

"It is the man of faith who is the man of duty."

" May we be able to spread our
Bibles on the mercy-seat, and
read them by the light of the
cloud of glory."

" I am a stranger in the
earth, hide not Thy com-
mandments from me."
PSALM cxix. 19.

25

THE WORD OF GOD

I OUGHT to put into practice in common
duties that saying "*Seek ye first the
kingdom of God.*" By the grace of God
and the strength of His Holy Spirit I desire
to lay down the rule not to speak to man
until I have spoken with God, not to do anything with my hand till I have been upon my
knees, not to read letters or papers until I
have read something of the Holy Scriptures.
I hope also to be able at "cool of the day,"
to pray and meditate upon the name of the
Lord. It may be an Eden here.

"Keep a grape of Eshcol beside you, and
moisten your parched palate with it when
you can ; and if you cannot get time for this,
then surely your Heavenly Father can refresh
you without it. You have been working for
Him all day. Go home singing of His love
to you that needed not your efforts to draw
it forth, nor any service directly done to His
name."

"Every line in this inspired Bible is wet
with the dew of the Spirit's love."

26

SEVENTH SUNDAY

"The sword of the Spirit—the sword which the Spirit uses. The sword is made up of various parts—the long blade, the handle. And so the Scriptures have many parts, but the Gospel is the sharp point by which it pierces the soul."

"A door is opened to you every time you apprehend one sentence or saying of the Lord's—a door in heaven, shall we say? a door like that of which John speaks (Rev. iv. 1), by which you are enabled in the Spirit to pass further into the secrets of God."

"Solomon-like wisdom is what we pray for in the knowledge of God, and Patmos-like revelation."

"Caleb lived very much on one promise for forty years."

"Use for yourself first what the Lord teaches you, and if He spare you, use it for others."

"When you have got a blessing take time to let it sink into your own heart before you tell it out."

"You say often 'If I pray I'll prosper.' That is only half the truth. If you meditate on the Word and pray, you will prosper."

"God gives us just a little at a time. He fed His Church on crumbs at first. Enoch lived on two crumbs of the bread of life, for all revealed Scripture then was, '*The seed of the woman shall bruise the head of the serpent*,' and '*Behold, the Lord cometh!*' But what a life he led on these two crumbs! And Noah in the ark with no more. How that man stood out against a whole world! O brethren, how the crumbs of the bread of life feed!"

"Lord, wean me from earth.
Lord, take me within the veil."

"When I awake I am still
with Thee."

PSALM cxxxix. 18.

WITHIN THE VEIL

July 6, 1857.

DREAMED last night that I was dying, and at the moment that I seemed about to depart I saw somewhere presented to me words that spoke of Christ's complete salvation. *Potentissimus*, I remember, was one, and it made me think upon Him who is able to save to the uttermost. There was another that spoke of His work for sinners, but I forget the word. It was a pleasant dream. May it be thus with me in stronger reality still when I come to die. I try to live upon this day by day.

April 28, 1866.

Sometimes of late I have felt as if I were almost standing on the step of the other world, my Father's house, with my face, however, toward this world, and that I might any moment be gently touched and drawn in within the veil.

January 27, 1867.

To-night and for some days past I have been feeling somewhat familiar with those that have gone within the veil, as if I could meet them and converse with them easily. "*For ever with the Lord*" is a word of joy ; sometimes it comes upon me like a bright flash, opening up for a moment the world beyond.

"'*These all died in faith*,' because they had lived in faith. Nay, it is still more expressive in the original—'*according to* their faith.' The faith that carried them through life carried them through death."

"We have boldness to enter into the holiest by the blood of Jesus. What more do we need in going into His presence ?"

"When death comes we may not be able to think at all, but it does not matter. He will keep us."

"Think upon the Lord while you can, and He will think upon you when you can't."

"The dying thief had nothing to think of but a dying Saviour. But a dying David and a dying Paul had nothing they cared to think upon but a dying Saviour."

"Preparation for death is almost an imagination. A believer does not prepare for death at all. Christ does it for him. The believer prepares for life."

"*The dead in Christ*"—a beautiful expression. It always reminds me of a mother with her dead infant lying on her bosom. Christ has His dead lying on His bosom, waiting for the resurrection."

"It is the Father's voice that says, ' *Blessed are the dead which die in the Lord* '—sleep in Jesus—and the Spirit's voice says, ' *Yea, Amen.* '"

"It was Christ, the second Adam, who first used the word Paradise."

"If we are in a right frame of mind we don't wish to die. It is no sign of a gracious person to be weary of life. Yet it is quite true that it is ' far better ' to depart and be with Christ ; ' far better ' than a Sabbath here, and a Monday to-morrow, and the business of the week to follow. But though this is true, we are taught to desire to remain here and serve Christ. It is only here we can pluck brands from the burning. Stay here and turn many to righteousness. Make it a rule not to think of death. Think of resurrection. Think of Christ's coming again. This is what sanctifies, what strengthens, what gladdens."

" Awake, awake, put on strength,
O arm of the Lord! that arm
that has plucked many a brand
from the burning, and has been
folded round many a lamb."

" Great and mighty things
which thou knowest not."

JER. xxxiii. 3.

SEEKING THE LOST

I FEAR much that I have been sliding into easy-minded contentment with the truth and the work going on, without seeing souls added every day. Delight in the Word read and preached is not the same thing as the light shining upon the dark world.

December 13, 1880.

" I long more and more to be filled with the Spirit, and to see my congregation moved and melted under the Word, as in great revival times, 'the place shaken where they are assembled together,' because the Lord has come in power."

" Write soon and tell me anything fitted to stir the soul in sleepy days. Do you ever feel that when there are no symptoms of converting work going on among your people your own soul gets ungirt for work ? I often find this, and I feel it at present."

" It is a peculiarity of the Divine rest that

34

it gives us intense rest, and at the same time intense restlessness for the souls of others."

"We are not only permitted to do good to those who are out of the way. We must do it if we are the Lord's people."

"God blesses those who do more than they are required to do."

"There is no lukewarmness in hell. There is no lukewarmness in heaven. Lukewarmness is found in the Church."

"I never like to hear any one say 'I never trouble others with my religion.' A believer must trouble others with his religion."

"Before you are saved you can do nothing to please God. After you are saved you cannot do enough to please Him."

"We may often do a great deal more by a silent look than by a volume of words."

"There is a reward for thinking upon His name (Mal. iii. 16). That is a quiet way of serving God, and open to every one."

"There is more originality in a full heart than in anything else."

"God knew what a wrench it would be for Philip to leave the great awakening in Samaria and go to meet one soul in the wilderness. So He sent His angel to tell him to go. It was as if Christ said to him, 'I left the ninety-and-nine in the wilderness to go to seek the one lost sheep. Go you and find that lost one in the desert.'"

"'*Without Me ye can do nothing.*' Christ has willed that the world should be influenced through the instrumentality of the Christian, so that as we say, 'Without *Him* we can do nothing,' He, as it were, says, 'Without *you* I can do nothing.'"

"If you say your hands are full, it is just what they ought to be."

" Let us not break the command
   that says, ' Cast thy burden on
   the Lord.' "

" He knoweth thy walking
through this great wilderness."

DEUT. ii. 7.

DAILY BURDENS

April 25, 1879.

THE Lord counts the days of the perfect man (Psa. xxxvii. 18), every day of his ordinary life, what it is, how it is to be spent, what it requires.

August 26, 1880.

One day alone here I found hid treasure in the words, " *the very hairs of your head are numbered*," all my family, all my classes, my texts, my writings, my sermons, my trials and cares.

" Jesus is our Servant in the upper sanctuary. He knows what we need, He thinks for us."

" Live one day at a time, no more. It is the burden of one day that the Lord carries. ' *Give us this day our daily bread.*' "

" Behold the fowls of the air, how merrily they sing, not troubled about next day's food or clothing. Be as they. Sing to your God and Father merrily to-day, and let the morrow take thought for itself."

"God puts care in our way, but He wants us to be without carefulness. He does not say, 'I will relieve you of a little care,' but 'I will leave no room for care.'"

"It is worth while coming to Christ even just to get rid of care, to sleep soundly and awake happy."

"The Lord does not vex and harass His people. If you are worried you are on the wrong way."

"Little daily worries are heaven-sent messengers to help you on the way home. What would you think of a sailor complaining of the wind that bears him homeward? A day spent among these worries is a day in God's school. One might say that the way to make the best of them is to make the least of them."

"A great feature of holiness is power to bear hard and heavy burdens."

"Burdens are part of a believer's education."

HEAVENLY SPRINGS

" We are to be rewarded not only for work done, but for burdens borne, and I am not sure but that the brightest rewards will be for those who have borne burdens without murmuring."

" God wants us to live a miniature life-time every day."

" Lord, give a heart to perceive
Thy giving."

"God opened her eyes, and
she saw a well of water."

GEN. xxi. 19.

THE WATER OF LIFE

GOT a great view of Rev. xxi. 6, Christ standing at the fountain and giving forth blessing δωρεάν, "freely." It was last night in reading the passage I saw Him so gracious. We have come to Him and been made righteous, and now He is continually giving, and will hand out to us blessing upon blessing. If we wonder, He will smile and say δωρεάν. If His love to us be expressed in marvellous fulness, and my soul feels it is utterly beyond expression why He should thus love me, He will smile and say δωρεάν. To-day I may stand with Him at the fountain, and ask "life more abundantly," and He will give it δωρεάν. I may ask joy and peace in believing. He will at once give it δωρεάν, not because of anything in me, but because of His own grace. Lord, I ask at this moment to be filled with the Holy Spirit, who will be in me always, showing the things of Christ, and raising intercession for others, and who will be to me "eye-salve." Thou wilt give all I ask δωρεάν. Thus, when I further ask blessing on my people, and upon my family, and upon the land also, even a new revival, will He not do it? I have no argument but one to use, and that is this most gracious word δωρεάν. When I get the crown from Him, the crown of righteousness, δωρεάν will be written upon it.

"Take the water of life freely, though you cannot allege a single reason why you should take it. Yet take it 'without a cause.'"

"Are there no conditions? Yes, there is one condition, thirst."

"No degree of love in you will ever make the gift freer than it is."

"It is a joy to God to give. It is a burden to Him to withhold. It is a grief to Him to carry about His gifts because we will not gladden Him by receiving them."

"'*If any man thirst.*' It is a great thing that Christ did not say for what. Fill up the blank and come to Him."

"Look into the fountain, and the very looking will make you thirsty."

"'*These things write we unto you, that your joy may be full.*' Here is a cry from the desert, from the lips of the beloved disciple, 'Found, found!' What have you found? 'A well of life! *Truly our fellowship is with the Father and with His Son Jesus Christ.*' This is the secret of joy."

"I often read at funerals the 21st chapter of Revelation, and I do it with this connection in my mind. There shall be no more sorrow, nor death, nor pain, nor crying, and '*I will give of the fountain of the water of life freely.*' I always feel that the Lord wanted to put these things within sight of one another. If we would draw more of the living water from the wells of salvation, we should have less sorrow. Drink more, believer! 'What aileth thee, Hagar? The well is just beside thee. Drink, and go on your way.'"

"Sit beside this well, and when your soul is sad because of sin *in* you, drink of this free love again. Sit beside this well, and when your soul is sad because of sin *around* you, drink of this well again. Sit there always, and when the coldness of blacksliding ones grieves you, drink of this well of free love again. Is it not a cure for every evil? Does it not also put hope and expectation into your soul? Sit there and pray on. Sit there and praise."

"O my God, never let me walk
even in the green pastures
without Thee!"

"The Lord is my portion,
saith my soul."

LAM. iii. 24.

December 6, 1874.

THE anniversary of my coming to Glasgow. I have now completed eighteen years in the city, and I was exactly eighteen years in the country. Who can tell what more remains? Christ is more than ever precious to me in His atonement, righteousness, merit, heart. Nothing else satisfies me. I only yearn to know Him better and preach Him more fully. His Cross and His Crown never lose their attractiveness. Day by day He is my rest, my heaven.

"I was meditating on two words to-day—'*He* was there *alone*.' It seems to me as if heaven would almost be sweeter if there were no multitudes even of angels, but Jesus only filling all."

"'*To me to live is Christ*.' Christ and life are one."

"'*To whom coming*'—the whole history of a believer's life."

"Wherever God is, something of heaven will be."

"If you have not two heavens you will never have one. If you have not a heaven here you will never have one yonder."

"'*This is My beloved Son, hear Him.*' It was worth while opening heaven to utter these words."

"Paul's experience was very much what he found in Christ, not what he found out about himself. This is the best of all experiences."

"The Lord is our dwelling-place, our home. We run away from all troubles outside and go home."

"'*The Lord Jesus Christ be with thy spirit.*' We often say 'Goodbye,' and others say 'Adieu,' but here is something more sweet and tender still to a friend of whom farewell is taken. It is 'Though I leave you, may Jesus Himself be with you.' Here is old Paul leaving young Timothy. They had often travelled together. They met at Lystra, and Paul '*would have him go forth with him*' (Acts xvi. 3), and so they went from city to city. They two, the young and the aged, met at Corinth, and when absent, Paul had sent a special message to him, so sweet was his company. But father and son are now to part, the sweet converse is over. Timothy is young, and may live long, but no more must Paul. 'However, happen what

may,' says he, 'may you have Christ for
your companion. Go through the wilderness with Him.' Paul had found Christ
enough, a treasure, a heaven. Paul had ever
found sympathy in Him, he never had to com-
plain of Jesus as he had of even Christian
friends (2 Tim. iv. 11–16), 'and O Timothy,
if you find in Him what I have found, all will
be well ! ' "

" ' *Jesus Christ is the same.*' He has
changed me, but He has never changed
Himself ! "

" May we give up our will to
Thine, and feel as if a burden
were lifted off us and laid on
Thee."

" It is enough for the disciple that he be as his
Master."

MATT. X. 25.

49

THE LOWEST PLACE

" WAS it to keep us from being ambitious like the disciples that He said of the labourers, ' *They received every man a penny* ' ? We are apt to seek to be great in the kingdom of heaven. I find it often difficult to be content to be *the least of all and servant of all*, to stand ever on the low step of free grace, without one quality or personal property to make a difference between me and the brand plucked from the burning at the last hour. We must exalt Christ so high as to get out of sight of ourselves in looking up to Him."

October 14, 1871.

My ambition now is very feeble compared with other days. To win souls and to know God more, and then to be in the kingdom, is all my desire.

" Don't be vexed because you are not first. We can't all be the eldest. Some one must be the youngest."

" The way to rise high in Christ's kingdom is to serve much."

" Angels will never be kings. They will always be servants."

" Some good people are very peremptory in asking God to give them souls. It may not be the best service you can do for God. The best service you can give Him is to submit to His will."

" Self-forgetting work is heavenly work."

" The best part of Christian work is that part which only God sees."

" Be content to let the Lord arrange how He is to give out His blessings, whether we get all we want or not."

" You need not be afraid of too much grace. Great grace never makes a man proud. A little grace is very apt to make a man puffed up. Be afraid of a little grace. Great grace never puffs up."

" We shall sit down *with* Abraham, Isaac, and Jacob in the kingdom, not *above* them, for they hoped in God while still in the shadows."

" ' *Many that are first shall be last.*' Even after the apostles had been endowed with the Holy Ghost at Pentecost they were outstripped by the young man Stephen. He outstripped the apostles, and he outstripped all the world. The whole of Jerusalem was shaken, and the enmity of the priests and scribes burst out. The apostles had never shone as the light, and they were let alone. There was one looking on that day at Stephen, very far behind the apostles, who soon became the first. He outstripped them all ; he shook all the world, as Stephen had shaken all Jeru-salem. It is all the gift of God's grace."

"Thou dost not give away the
children's bread. Surely, then,
Thou keepest it for the children. Give it now to us."

"Can God furnish a table
in the wilderness?"

PSALM lxxviii. 19.

53

THE LORD'S DAY

October 1, 1843.

I WISH to pray from this date every Sabbath morning before going out to preach, and every time I go to preach to stand still a little and praise the Lord for sending to sinners His glorious gospel.

October 4, 1873.

I now try to pray every Sabbath before leaving the pulpit : " Lord, give fruit, forgive the sin ; fill me with the Spirit again and again, and accept my praise."

" I preached lately on the love of the Father—one of the sweetest days I ever had in my life ! The common truth seemed so fresh and so pleasant to the taste."

" Yesterday I felt a little of abounding grace, and the blessedness of being sure yet to be holy, holy, holy. It seemed a very short day—the sun 'hasted to go down,' I thought. We would need a long eternity, or heaven would be no heaven, it would be so soon over."

FOURTEENTH SUNDAY

"If the word everlasting were not in our salvation, in our righteousness, we would be unsatisfied with it all. If 'everlasting' were not written over the joys of heaven, we would be trembling lest the banquet should have an end, lest the day should have an evening."

"When breezes from Lebanon blow, what a world the eternal world appears, and what a Lord is the Lord of glory!"

"There is joy even in happy heaven when a sinner is saved, so that every Sabbath heaven is getting happier, because lost souls are being found."

"God can do more on earth than in heaven for the glory of His name."

"Jesus did not need to say more than 'There am I' to make His disciples come together. They liked to be where He was. How the presence of the mother sitting by adds to the children's joy at their play! So it is with Christ and His disciples. 'In the midst.' He is the very soul and heart of the meeting. In the worship above, the Lamb is in the midst of the throne."

"'They that feared the Lord spake often one to another, and the Lord . . . heard.' He listened, and He marked down the attendance, to be put in His book of remembrance. A congregation of true worshippers is just a congregation of those who think upon the Lord."

" In the Book of Psalms we have four outstanding references to the altar, and in them we see—(1) the true worshipper (xxvi. 6); (2) the troubled worshipper (xliii. 3, 4); (3) the worshipper travelling on his way to Zion (lxxxiv. 3); (4) the triumphant worshipper (cxviii. 27)."

"Change me, Lord, from glory
to glory, into Thine image, till
glory come."

"Thou shalt make them
drink of the river of
Thy pleasures."

PSALM xxxvi. 8.

57

THE JOY OF THE LORD

February 22, 1846.

I HAVE been taught that joy in the Spirit is the frame in which God blesses us to others. Joy arises from fellowship with Him — I find that whatever sorrow or humiliation of spirit presses on us, that should give way in some measure to a fresh taste of God's love when going forth to preach.

September 8, 1849.

Seeking the "*joy unspeakable*" at its fountainhead; "*In Whom believing.*"

"I was much struck to-day by a simple thought, namely, 'Our joys are only beginning.' Yes, the joys we have tasted are mere foretastes. All we get here is but an earnest, and no more. And then, as truly as our joys are only beginning, so our sorrows are ending. They will soon be over, our last tear shed, our last sigh heaved, the last wrinkle on our brow smoothed away by the hand that places on our head the crown of glory. 'Come, Lord Jesus!'"

FIFTEENTH SUNDAY

" ' Rejoice ! ' is as much a command as
' Repent ! ' "

" Cultivate joy as much as you cultivate
honesty and uprightness."

" The oil of joy calms down the waves of
trouble."

" Why should we be afraid to rejoice
when God is not afraid to trust us with
joy ? "

" We are strange creatures. There is
nothing we want more than joy, and yet
when the cup is put within our reach we
shrink from taking more than a few drops.
The Holy Ghost wants us to drink the cup
of blessing to the dregs."

" Love is the motive for working. Joy is
the strength for working."

" Would it have been right for the prodigal
to sit at the table dropping tears into his
cup, saying, ' I can't be glad,' when the
Father said, ' *It is meet that we should make
merry and be glad* ' ? "

" ' *Continue ye in My love.*' Live in the
sunshine."

" Love and joy are the two prominent
fruits of the Spirit. If you can cherish this
glad spirit you will be a useful witness,
though you should never say a word. Try
never to have a frown on your brow."

" ' *Filled with all joy and peace.*' If He

59

fill you with this, there will be no room for anything earthly."

"There are far more people made to think by seeing a believer's joy than by any words he may speak."

"I hope you have been going on your way singing some more notes of the 'new song,' tuning your hearts for the Hallelujah chorus at the coming of the Lord with all His saints. It is a small matter to make heaven ring with song; the glorious honour given us is to make this very wilderness, this valley of Baca, this earth under the curse, ring and ring again with our joyful burst of praise to our unseen but much-loved Lord, the King of kings!"

"Visit us with Thy salvation—
for there are folds and folds of
the robe of righteousness that
we would fain have Thee to
unfold to us."

"I will love him and manifest Myself to him."

JOHN xiv. 21.

GOD IN CHRIST

February 18, 1872.

I FIND my Lord and Saviour more and more satisfying to my soul. In very deed He is all my salvation and all my desire.

April 10, 1880.

It is a time of great political excitement. But I am less moved now by all such changes; my time on earth may be soon finished. The atoning blood is more than ever precious to me. The righteousness of Christ is more than ever glorious in my view. Christ Himself is altogether lovely.

"I can hardly believe that man is a Christian who does not every day betake himself to the atoning work of Christ."

"If you can do without the blood you are a backslider."

"Do not try to put religion in the place of Christ. The heart of religion is to know Christ, and to know Him better, and to know Him still better. Then to see Him as He is, and then to be made like Him."

SIXTEENTH SUNDAY

" Many want salvation, but they do not want the Saviour."

" Each plant needs a whole sun, and each of us needs a whole Saviour."

" Salvation is not fleeing to the shadow of the Great Rock. It is fleeing to the Man who is our Hiding-place, and laying our head on His bosom."

" Christ does not say, ' I will show you the way,' but ' *I am the Way*.' He does not merely say, ' I will give you bread of life,' but He says, ' *I am the Bread of Life*.' "

" A God not seen through Christ is no God at all."

" Draughts of the water of life are just fresh views of Christ."

" The Good News takes the sting out of all that men call evil tidings."

" ' *Delight thyself also in the Lord*.' In the midst of Paradise with all its wondrous beauty, if God Himself had not come and walked with Adam in the cool of the day it would not have been a very happy place, for unfallen man's delight was in God Himself. His gifts would not supply His place. We have lost Paradise, but we have not lost the Lord. We have got back our joy, though we have not yet got back Paradise. We can find all that will make us happy in Him. It is meeting with the Lord personally, face to face, that gives rest. The blood gives the conscience rest, but the heart craves something more, and that is fellowship with Him who gave us that atoning blood and sprinkled it on our souls."

> " Teach that troubled tempted
> one how to handle the shield
> of faith."

" Say to them that are of
a hasty heart, Be strong,
fear not ! "

ISA. xxxv. 4 (marg.).

THE SHIELD OF FAITH

July 24, 1842.

I NEVER felt my entire want of all good so much as now, so that never till now could I so truly cry, "*in my flesh, no good thing.*"

August 20, 1878.

I see that faith is high just when our thoughts about our Lord Himself are high and great and satisfying. It was thus with the centurion, and he went away with his prayer fully granted.

"Any marks of a rising tide? I long to come into the track of some trade-wind from heaven that would send us sooner homeward to breathe amid the realities of a better world. Is there not honey in this verse, '*Christ is the end of the law for righteousness*'? Hold Him up as the true fulfiller of our ministry.

"Only get above the clouds, brother. We must think only of how the Lord may be glorified. '*None of us liveth to himself.*' Never mind vigour or want of vigour, comfort or want of comfort in our preaching and ministry. All we have to do is to do our best as we get strength at the time, and, as Robert M'Cheyne used to say, 'the Lord can show us how to catch fish with a broken net.'

"'Be of good cheer.' Our works do not save us, our ill-success will not destroy us, our corruptions and imperfections will only make us more indebted to Jesus for ever. '*He that believeth shall be saved.*'"

"Keep your face toward the sun and you will not see the shadows behind."

"We should take our discouragements as means of grace."

"Christ utilises even the backslidings of His people for their further good."

"The Lord sometimes needs to lift us above our lawful comforts, and sometimes, too, He needs to lift us above our spiritual enjoyments."

"Faith makes giants look like grasshoppers, and unbelief makes grasshoppers look like the Anakim. Unbelief looks at the difficulty, and faith looks at God."

"Remember, the fig-tree has written upon it, '*Have faith in God.*'"

"God fills our hands with work, but He does not overburden us. When we are overburdened it is time for us to stop."

"It is faith, not feeling, leaning, not resolving, that carries us through."

"Doubts and fears are not marks of God's children. They are remnants of the old nature, specks on the eye of faith. You should give them no quarter."

"When we are united to Christ we can say, 'I am in Christ,' as well as, 'Christ is in me.' My faith need have no ups and downs, for my righteousness is in heaven. I may lose my sight of it, but it is there all the same. There is the boat on the Lake of Galilee. Dark night is coming on, and the disciples are in danger. Let us suppose two angels are looking on, and one says, 'There are the Master's disciples, and they are in sore trouble.' 'There is no fear,' the other says. 'They are the Master's property. He is on the mountain praying for them.' In a little while they see the Master leave the mountain, walk over the sea, and come into the boat. 'Ah,' they say, 'it is impossible they can sink now. He is in the boat with them.'"

" The clouds which have arisen
from the marshes of our sins
need new bursts of the Sun of
righteousness to melt them
away. Shine forth! Shine
forth!"

"Thou hast forgiven the
iniquity of Thy people,
Thou hast covered all
their sin."

PSALM lxxxv. 2.

GOD AND THE SINNER

TRYING to-day, the anniversary of my
first sermon as ordained minister, to
review the past, and to spend every hour, so
far as I have leisure, in prayer for more grace.
I am greatly struck with 2 Tim. iii. 2 :
" *unthankful, unholy,*" as characteristics of pro-
fessing formalists in the last days ; but as in
another form applicable to myself. Shame
and sorrow fill me at my unholiness, after all
the kindness of the Lord, opportunities, privi-
leges, seasons of communion, example of
other saints, blessings sent. Lord, give,
give !

December 23, 1880.

I got a most humbling discovery of two
things : that I had exceedingly little of that
quality of a true minister—" beseeching "—
and exceeding little real belief or realising of
the greatness of eternal death, and the judg-
ment upon sinners.

" Sin is the mark for God's arrows."
" No sinner has ever yet borne all that his

sins deserved. Only Christ in the room of sinners has borne all that was due for sin. This is the blessedness of the saved man. The sinner who comes under the shadow of the Cross has borne all that was due for sin."

"Sin forgotten is not sin forgiven. It is only the postponement of the trial and the sentence."

"If deep sorrow and remorse for sin could blot out sin, hell would be a great Calvary."

"The natural heart keeps no record of sin. It is only God's law which does so."

"God does not say 'Pay what you can,' but 'Pay what you owe.'"

"There are some men who will not believe they are sinners till they are in hell."

"Men speak of the dignity of human nature. There is no dignity in a lost sinner. The dignity of human nature is to be reconciled to God."

"No one who is anxious to have a Saviour has committed the unpardonable sin."

"Sinners in Christ Jesus are saints."

"It is no burden to God to uphold worlds. Sin is the only thing that is a burden to Him."

"It is not by looking on your bruise that you will be sanctified, but by looking on Him that was bruised for you. It is not by smiting on your breast that you will grow holy, but by looking on Him who was smitten for you."

"Power over habits of sin may be gained by confessing sin.

> " ' He breaks the power of cancell'd sin,
> He sets the prisoner free.'

We can also say—

> ' He breaks the power of sin confess'd,
> And gives the victory.' "

" When anything intercepts our
view of Christ, may we feel
what loneliness is."

"I know Whom I have
believed."
2 Tim. i. 12.

FAITH AND FEELING

May 30, 1868.

R EVIEWING the past I see this fact in my life worthy of continual admiration and thanks, that for more than thirty years I have never been shaken in my quiet resting on the Lord Jesus. I have been many, many times unhappy for a time, but never led to doubt my interest in the Lord Jesus. The Lord has never let my eyes close to the one foundation. He has kept me from mixing up my feeling with Christ's work. It has been all of grace, the doing of the Spirit who takes the things of Christ and shows them.

" Nothing makes assurance so sure as knowing that God gets honour by accepting a sinner."

"It is faith growing up into assurance that gives real peace."

"Faith grows upon the soil of felt sin."

"It is the privilege and the duty of believers looking at the blood not to have a fear or a doubt. You can't honour God more, you can't please the Holy Spirit more, or Christ more, than by putting unbounded confidence in the blood."

"Assurance is not a privilege only, but a duty."

"The youngest believer is entitled to full assurance."

"If at any time we lose the sense of His presence, the way to get it back is not by sitting down to 'count our evidences.' It is by coming back to Him."

"Feelings have nothing to do with justification. They are a part of sanctification."

"You will never have feeling till you have faith."

"Feeling is not to be trusted. Fear may drive away all feeling. Faith by itself is not to be trusted. Our standing fast is due to a living, interceding Saviour, and our eye must rest on Him in an hour of trial."

"Faith is no more a part of the Gospel than your eye is part of the light of the sun."

"Some anxious souls may wish that Christ had given us a definition of faith. But He does not. He says 'have it,' but He does not explain what it is. He wants us to look up, and not in—to look at the object of faith, and not to the act of faith."

"When we weep over Christ's sufferings merely because they are sad and sorrowful, that is feeling. When we weep because of the sin that made Him suffer, and see that He suffered for *us*, that is faith."

"It is not the amount of knowledge we have that saves. It is the use we make of that knowledge."

"Holy Spirit, sanctify me by old sorrow."

"Nevertheless, afterward."

HEB. xii. 11.

THE CHASTENING OF THE LORD

I FEAR Satan is watching me and trying to get me to put sorrow in the place of prayer. This seems to be my time for glorifying and serving the Lord by bearing and suffering, as formerly by active doing. Lord, may I not fail now !

"We must learn more and more how to suffer. '*Thy will be done*' is one of the heavenly plants that Jesus left the seed of when He was here. We must cultivate it in our gardens. And so also there is another. '*The Lord thinketh upon me*,' a plant cultivated by King David when he was an exile in the wilds of Engedi. This plant is the believer's 'Forget-me-not.'"

"The Master bore the Cross of atonement that He might make us righteous. He leaves us a cross of our own that we may be made holy."

"There may be real submission to the will of God while we can't help wishing things were otherwise. God does not ask us to feel that everything is for the best, but He does ask us to believe it."

"It is worth while being wounded to have the hands of that Physician upon you."

"A believer is an Æolian harp, and every event of his life is just the passing wind drawing out the music. And God hears it."

"We have got more from Paul's prison-house than from his visit to the third heavens."

"'*He will not suffer you to be tempted above that ye are able.*' He meant you to feel the stress and weight of the trial, but He never meant you to be crushed under it. There is majesty here. '*He will not suffer.*' He will not allow Satan to tempt you too much. Be of good cheer. You will never fall under any temptation. You will be inexcusable if you sink under any load."

There is fulness of sympathy in our God. The river that flows from the throne of God and of the Lamb, did you ever hear of it drying up? The "*Father of mercies and the God of all comfort.*" The Son, the "Consolation of Israel," He that was sent to comfort all that mourn; the Holy Spirit "the Comforter," leading us to the Consolation of Israel and the Father of mercies. We are at the deep, deep well of love. The weariest head and the sorest heart may lean on the bosom on which the beloved disciple leaned, and find indescribable relief and indescribable sympathy, for He will whisper all the time, "*All things work together for good to them that love God.*" "*For though He cause grief, yet will He have compassion according to the multitude of His mercies.*"

" O shine forth, shine forth in my
spirit, that I may feel Thy love
to me filling my heart."

"I shall be satisfied when
I awake, with Thy like-
ness."

PSALM xvii. 15.

CONSTRAINING LOVE

January 1, 1853.

I DO love the Lord ; there is none in heaven but He, none on earth whom my whole soul goes forth unto, and never may it rest but in enjoying Him.

July 4, 1860.

I want to live in the love of God, for God, enjoying God, glorifying God, and every day able to tell what new discovery I have made in the fulness of Christ.

July 28, 1872.

Christ in the circle of His disciples would make them so happy that none would remark upon the want of John or Peter. Christ as *" Lamb in the midst of the throne "* is able to give intense joy to millions upon millions, His look, voice, smile, presence. Oh to see *" the King in His beauty ! "* We shall be sick of love, and yet find all health in that love. *" All my springs are in Thee."*

" It will be ecstasy to have made this

attainment, to love the Lord our God with all our heart and soul and strength and mind."

"Those who have real love to Christ always wish they had more."

"Of all things beware of a cold heart."

"Christ will not let anything interfere with your love for Him. He says, 'I am all for you, and you must be all for Me.'"

"'Jealousy' expresses the peculiar sensitiveness of Divine love."

"Our one great hindrance to fuller blessing is something along with God in our heart."

"*The love of Christ constraineth us*" (2 Cor. v. 14). There never was a ship that went so swiftly and straightly to its destination as did Paul. He never turned aside. His eye was always fixed on Christ, and he could think of nothing else, night and day, but this Saviour. He was always thinking what he could do for Him, and when that was done, what next he could do. He seemed sometimes to go even beyond measure. He says to the Corinthians, "I know you sometimes think me beside myself." This love was so present to Paul that it was quite easy for him to leave everything. He said, "You need not pity me. I count all things but loss for Christ's sake." He was entranced with Christ's beauty. He was fairly taken captive by His love. You find him in prison. What is he doing? Smiling and singing. Look at him in ship-wreck—as cheery as on dry land. This love was like an atmosphere round him. You remember Jacob's love for Rachel, how he served seven years for her, and felt nothing hard, for he was always within hearing of the music of her voice, of the sound of her foot-step. Is it not so with us if we love Christ?

" May we so enjoy communion
with Thee that when we lose it
we may feel just as if we were
away from our home."

" The way into the holiest
of all."

HEB. ix. 8.

WALKING WITH GOD

January 30, 1857.

IN hour by hour living in fellowship I greatly fail, and yet I prize it above all things. I would fain work under an ever-open heaven, and say every hour with Stephen, " *Behold, I see the heavens open, and the Son of man.*"

May 31, 1844.

" My soul gets weary. O to be as those above who seem to grow holier and stronger by every act they do in their heavenly service ! ' *His servants shall serve Him,*' and all the while they 'see His face,' and His name becomes brighter on their foreheads. They get more and more of the look and air of true children of such a Father."

" Be thou in the fear of the Lord all the day long. Keep under the light that beams from Jacob's ladder, and you will always have a Bethel-fear."

" Walking with God is life-habit."

" Elijah had such fellowship with God that he could say, ' *God, before Whom I stand.*'

Gabriel could not say more than that when he came down in after-days."

" Fellowship with God answers a thousand questions of casuistry."

" ' *Because he hath set his love upon Me*'— ' *Because he hath known My name*'—the two folding doors of the secret place of the Most High."

" We don't need to retire to the desert to meet with God. It is God who meets with us, and He can come to us at our ordinary duties."

" If you want to be used and sent on messages for the Lord, live near Him."

" It is because saints are in such a poor condition for work that so few souls are saved."

" He treats thy selfishness as one of thy sins, a sin for the Fountain."

" ' *Partakers of the Divine nature.*' What an end to all corruption ! We shall not know ourselves."

" Sloth and self-indulgence are far worse than persecution. They make faith dwindle to a shadow. If you could give your life for Christ, will you not live your life for Him ?

" Weakness is no excuse for sloth. Our talent must not be hid in a napkin."

" Christ Jesus came into the world to save sinners. He is coming into the world again to save saints, that is, to give them the full salvation, and to show how He can make brighter than the angels those who were sunk so low as to be chief of sinners."

"The believer sits loose to all earthly things, ready to ascend like Elijah, if the Lord were to send the fiery chariot for him to-day."

"Grace in us is just the impress of God's grace upon our souls."

"If you were to say, 'Am I a man greatly beloved?' He would answer, '*As the Father hath loved Me, so have I loved you.*'"

" Let my will be one with the
Lord's, falling into that great
stream as a tributary."

" The manifold grace of
God."
1 PETER iv. 10.

April 24, 1847.

OUR praying for all saints must be very important, probably because it is our seeking the place we desire for all alike, and so asking what may be very widely useful.

February 15, 1868.

I learned one thing over again, that while the Lord seems to use evangelists to awaken souls, He keeps a place for older labourers, in the instruction and leading of the saved. We must all know our own place, and be satisfied. We are while here, like roots under ground with all the principles of life, struggling upward, and soon to shoot forth above many a leaf of beauty, and many a branch bearing fruit worthy of Him in whom our root is fastened. The clods of earth interrupt our upward growth for a time. What a burst of sunshine and glorious liberty awaits us!

" In my usual reading I have come to 1 Corinthians, and there have been led to notice one interesting feature in Paul.

Though the greatest and wisest—best-stored of all—he never seems to like to stand alone. It is always Paul and Timothy—Paul and Barnabas—Paul and Titus—Paul and Sosthenes. Now this is not from want of firmness, needing the sympathy of others to decide him, but from deep wisdom. He sees that this is God's way of keeping the workers humble. He does not employ one only at a building, but several, and so no one can say, 'The success is owing to me.' It may be your fellow-labourer that is the secret of the blessing ; perhaps he is more prayerful than you, more single-minded."

"It is a rule in the family of God that every one that loveth Him that begat loveth him also that is begotten of Him. We are to work together."

"When grace comes into the heart of a man the instinct for sympathy grows stronger, and, on the other hand, it prompts him to give more sympathy."

"In holiness we must go on together, not alone. You will not get on by separating yourself to read and pray. It must be along 'with them that call on the Lord.' We are to climb Pisgah together, and from the top see the stretch of the land. But we are not to go alone."

" God loves unity, and so He loves a united cry, a petition signed by more than one."

"Christ liked to come to the Feast when He was going to give blessing. He liked to come to the upper room, when they were all assembled there."

" When believers can work together, overlooking each others' faults and failings, then the blessing comes. The dew does not fall on a windy night; it is when all is still."

"If we are true disciples we are always learning. Every disciple we meet with has something for us, if we could only get it. We are wrong if we are not trying to draw out of others what God has given them. Never think you can be of no use to another disciple. God does not give everything to one. Aquila and Priscilla could do a great deal even for Apollos."

" 'Exhort one another daily.' If the two Emmaus disciples had been silent would Jesus have come between ? "

" Crush our hearts between these
two millstones—a sense of sin,
and a sense of Divine grace."

" The exceeding riches of
His grace."

EPH. ii. 7.

93

RICHES OF GRACE

SOME glimpses of free grace, seeing the Lord to be giving, giving, giving all around from year to year, in things spiritual and temporal, seeing that we do nothing but take, take, take.

July 20, 1872.

A day much spent in crying to the Lord. For myself, I could ask Eph. iii. 17, 20, but what a thought ! I myself ἐρριζωμένος ἐν ἀγάπῃ, and then enabled to comprehend something of love's depth, length, breadth, and *to know* the love which goes beyond knowledge. All this I can plead for, and two grounds of pleading came up before me. His riches of glory might move Him the more by contrast to pity me in my poverty as I speak with Him. Then also He can do this without going beyond His already begun means, " *according to the power that is at work in us.*"

" No man is a disciple till he has a heart experience of what *grace* means. A man awakened is not a disciple. He may fall asleep again. The desire for grace is not grace."

"Judge of God's love only by His unspeakable gift—a gift irrevocably given and given to you—never by frames and states and feelings and your own thoughts."

"The promises are streams coming down from the heart of Christ."

"Christ never seems to be able to keep to Himself what He gets. He always gives it away."

"God is able to love us without a cause though we hated Him without a cause."

"You must have misunderstood God or you would have been drawn to Him long ago."

"God longs for your company. *'Return unto Me, for I have redeemed thee.'* "

" *'The Lord hear thee in the day of trouble.'* The Lord might say to us, 'Ah, when there was no storm you took your own way. Now in the tempest you cry to Me.' It is a beautiful thing about the Lord that He knows our selfishness, but never upbraids us for it, if we come to Him."

"Christ met His disciples on a mountain in Galilee, and what did He say to them? Did He upbraid them? Did He say to them, 'I will never trust you again'? To those very men who had so ungratefully forsaken Him and fled, He said, '*Go ye into all the world and preach the Gospel to every creature.* I will trust even you with My message to the sinner.' Herein is Christ's love."

"Did not John the beloved disciple flee with the rest and forsake his Master? And did his Master upbraid him? He treated him next day as His bosom friend, giving His mother into his care."

"' *Go tell My brethren.*' He is not ashamed to call them brethren though they were ashamed to call Him Lord a few days ago!"

" When we pray in the morning
to be filled with the Spirit, may
we expect to be filled all day
with thoughts of Christ."

" The secret of the Lord is
with them that fear Him."

PSALM XXV. 14.

97

LIGHTS IN THE WORLD

January 3, 1842.

ON looking back I am grieved and vexed, most of all at my few hours of real prayer all this year. How little have I done for God in the Spirit! I feel myself a very dim-shining light; a vessel much soiled.

September 16, 1851.

In prayer in the wood for some time, having set apart three hours for devotion; felt drawn out much to pray for that peculiar fragrance which believers have about them, who are very much in fellowship with God. It is like an aroma, unseen but felt. Other Christians have the beauty of the Rose of Sharon. These have the fragrance too.

"When God comes to a man He does not only say, 'Arise, receive!' but 'Arise, shine!'"

"If you shine as lights now and cast your light on the darkness around you you will hear of it in the ages to come. If you do not, God will get others to do it."

TWENTY-FIFTH SUNDAY

"No loveliness, believer! Yet you are grafted on the stem of the Rose of Sharon!"

"If you are filled with the Spirit God will use everything about you, the tones of your voice, even the putting out of your hand."

"There are some people who would be offended if it were questioned that they were Christians, and who yet would not care to be called 'sons of God.' Why is this? Perhaps because there is more expected of a son than of a servant."

"Jesus says to His disciples, '*Ye are the light of the world.*' Paul seemed to feel this so awfully solemn that he was allowed, we may say, to soften it when he wrote to the Philippians, '*Ye shine as lights in the world.*' But Christ's words are stronger."

"When you have been catching the far-off notes of the multitude around the throne, have you not said, '*My leanness, my leanness, woe unto me!*' Or when you have been reading about being blessed with '*all spiritual blessings in Christ,*' have you not said to yourself, 'My leanness, my leanness!' Or when you have been musing on that name Christ gives His people, 'light of the world,' have you not said, 'Poor light, if I am the light.' You feel almost ashamed as you read of being a joint-heir with Christ, and think, 'Has Christ no better representative on earth

than me ? ' You may be blameless in the
eyes of men, but you feel inwardly you are
not Christlike. You feel you need to go
back to the first principles of the oracles of
God."

" Lord, touch again my sight, that
I may see farther than before."

"Then were the disciples
glad when they saw the
Lord."

JOHN xx. 20.

JOY AND PEACE IN BELIEVING

I HAVE been asking calm faith, burning love, deep peace, bright hope, true compassion for souls, glowing zeal for God's glory.

Yesterday evening my desires were : one drop of the atoning blood to give me continuous deep peace ; one drop of the oil of gladness to give my heart all the gladness I could wish ; one look of His uplifted countenance to strengthen and sanctify, drawing me to Himself ; one breathing of His Spirit to pour in fresh life through my whole being.

"Faith looks within the veil, it does not stop at the blue sky."

"Our heaven is up yonder with God. God's heaven is down here upon earth with us. His delights are with the sons of men."

"It is not ceasing to do evil and learning to do well only that sanctifies us. It is breathing the atmosphere of the love of Christ."

TWENTY-SIXTH SUNDAY

"The joy of holiness is often sweeter than the joy of forgiveness, for the joy of holiness implies fellowship with God."

"'*My peace I give unto you*'—the peace of God-man when He had finished His work."

"Peace is the mantle dropped by Christ."

"'*Peace be unto you!*' Christ has made peace, and He brings it to the disciples—the first-ripe sheaves to the upper room. How sweet they would be! Again He says, '*Peace be unto you!*' It is the 'peace, peace' of Isaiah xxvi."

"'*Keep yourselves in the love of God.*' This is the grand remedy for care. It is our safety in the midst of comfort. It sets our affection on things above. It is the secret of a holy life. It takes away the sting of affliction. God's method of showing His love may alter, but it is the same love."

"Winds from every quarter are stilled by 'Peace' from His lips."

"The 22nd Psalm is the Good Shepherd purchasing peace for us. The 23rd Psalm is the peace He has purchased."

"'Make your peace with God' is a very delusive expression. You take peace; you don't make it."

"'*These things write we unto you that your joy may be full.*' 'It has filled my heart,' John says, 'and it will fill yours.' Nothing in the world will fill your heart. You may get a little from earthly things, but if you want gladness to fill your heart, you must get it in fellowship with the Lord Jesus. 'All mankind by the fall lost communion with God,' but here it is restored. John often uses His Master's words, and this is one of them. '*These things have I spoken unto you that My joy might remain in you, and that your joy might be full.*' You need not lose it. It fills the heart, and it remains."

" '*He is our peace.*' A copy of the inscription upon Gideon's altar."

"Let us be as watchful after the victory as before the battle."

"And commanded the porter to watch."

MARK xiii. 34.

WATCHING UNTO PRAYER

January 2, 1848.

I SIN against the Lord by labouring more than I pray.

April 27, 1855.

I discover that very small distractions may become very great temptations.

March 16, 1878.

Have been noticing that it is not so good to reserve prayer and praise for such times as the beginning and end of work, as it is to interweave those into the work as it goes on. The heart is thus kept continually watchful, looking upward.

February 3, 1888.

Incessant work seems to me to be more than ever a snare, hindering prayer in several ways. There is great need of "*watching unto prayer.*"

"Whenever you don't care to cry for help

you are not watching. Watching and praying always go together."

"Always follow your work with believing prayer."

"Would you not for your own sake be *'perfect and complete in all the will of God'*? Then remember what goes before—*'always labouring fervently in prayers.'* "

"Have we not sometimes prayed for blessings and then forgotten all about them? Long afterwards the answer to these prayers came. God did not forget them, though we did."

"Hezekiah's prayer got a large answer. When you send in a petition to the Lord leave a wide margin, that He may write a great deal on it."

"When you find a promise it will not fall into your lap. You must shake the tree by prayer."

"Real earnest prayer is hard work. There are so many interruptions, so many excuses. A believing man is more ready at work than at prayer. Satan has a special ill-will to praying people. Some one has said that Satan's orders are, 'Fight not with small nor great, but only with the king of Israel.' Fight not with that saint nor that other, but only with the praying people."

"I never remember in the course of my

ministry meeting with any one who wanted
to give up part of his work because he was
going to take the time for prayer. If any
one did do this, the part of work he had left
would soon be filled up."

"It is not right for God's people to say
when a matter for prayer is put before them,
'Oh, what can my prayers do?' What can
your God do?"

"The seven thousand praying ones in the
days of Elijah had prayed out seven thousand
fighting men into the field for Israel's de-
liverance (1 Kings xx. 15 ").

"Let us form right conceptions
of God gracious and merciful,
causing grace and mercy to
find their way between the
banks of truth and righteousness."

"I will behold Thy face in
righteousness."

PSALM xvii. 15.

THE LORD OUR RIGHTEOUSNESS

July 26, 1862.

LAST night went to sleep repeating " the Lord my righteousness," and feeling as if with this upon my forehead I could go into the New Jerusalem and to the just.

"Are you more weary than ever of your own righteousness—of self, which is truly a hydra—of your fellow-men and corruption ? Are you not ' *looking for and hasting unto the coming of the day of God* ' ? You and I shall then stand in our Redeemer's beauty, all fair, no spot, without blemish, without wrinkle, white and clean, in fine linen, in garments of needlework, *like Jesus*. Will you know me in that day ? Will you know yourself ? "

"The believers' safety is secured by the righteousness of God. Righteousness demands that we should be welcomed into the inheritance. The Lord, the Righteous Judge, shall put the crown on our head on that day."

"A sinner must begin with righteousness, not with love."

"God gives no peace but by righteousness."

"Christ's obedience was His taking up our undone work."

"His life of obedience—you know what it was. A walk from Bethlehem to Calvary without a stumble."

"Christ came to provide us with righteousness undefiled. He obeyed for us perfectly. In that robe He walked through our world every day, and when He had finished His walk, as Elijah left his mantle to Elisha, the Saviour left His robe for us to wear."

"Righteousness and love constitute grace."

"You can remember when you thought you were to get into heaven in spite of God's holiness. Now you know that it is because of His holiness that you get there, for none but the all-holy God would have sent His Son to die for us, or would have known that only a perfectly holy heaven could make us happy to all eternity. Once you dreaded holy ground—but now holy ground is become to you as the very floor of heaven."

"Propitiation is not only appeasing wrath, but it is, so to speak, drawing out favour."

"Christ's holy human nature did not know how *not* to obey and how *not* to suffer when the Father required it of Him."

HEAVENLY SPRINGS

" The man who believes on the Lord Jesus keeps all the ten commandments."

" Until you can build your hope for eternity on the two tables of the law unbroken, you can have no solid peace."

"Give a larger heart and a holier
to me."

"From glory to glory."
2 COR. iii. 18.

GRACE AND GLORY

February 4, 1855.

MY knowledge of Christ seems to me at this day like as if a man saw about his own length all round him, while mist rested as an atmosphere upon the horizon, the sun just faintly struggling through. When that mist rolls off, what a scene, what a discovery of glory !

November 3, 1856.

Though I find it difficult often to realise myself chief of sinners, yet I never feel that difficulty in another respect. I am chief of debtors.

" I was greatly refreshed yesterday by two words from the mouth of the Lord in the verse, '*For a small moment have I forsaken thee, but with great mercies will I gather thee*' (Isa. liv. 7). The words are חֶסֶד עוֹלָם 'the mercy of an eternity.' What is this that is coming to us, brother ? The mercy of a whole eternity ! "

" When God sought a ransom for us He

took all the payment out of this treasury, Himself."

"The Ransom-money is the only current coin at the court of heaven, and it has the resurrection stamp upon it. We used to speak of 'a king's ransom,' but guess if you can what the value must be of a Ransom that sets free nations, kingdoms, peoples."

"Judah had a rich land for his inheritance, but Levi had a rich God."

"If you ask me what is glory? Well, I can't tell you, but I know that it is a hundred times better than grace."

"When Jesus tells us of the glory and beauty of the New Jerusalem, lest we should think it incredible that feet like ours should ever tread the golden streets, or hands like ours ever pluck the fruit of the tree of life, or lips like ours ever taste the water of that pure river, He says, ' John, write. *These sayings are faithful and true.*'"

"God is not ashamed to be called our God, but over and above that He hath prepared for us a city, and we may be sure this city is worthy of God. It will be a city that will make us say, '*Behold how He loved us!*'"

"We are all alike cleansed by the same atoning blood, we all have the same precious faith, but some go further on than others, and get nearer God. It is simply the Spirit enabling some to make more use of the sprinkled blood than others. Some are contented to get into the place of safety. Others want to press farther up the hill. '*We have boldness to enter into the holiest by the blood of Jesus,*' but some don't use it, and they stay at a distance. Moses and Joshua went higher than the seventy elders, but they needed no more warrant to go up than they had—the sprinkled blood. Now that we have liberty to go to God, let us go in. As Paul puts it, '*Let us draw near.*' Let us go to the top of the hill, and enter the cloud of glory, and speak with God there."

" If our hands that should grasp the heavenly treasures are kept closed because they are filled with earthly things, deal with us, Lord, until we stretch out empty hands, suppliants for Thy blessings."

" He suffered thee to hunger."

DEUT. viii. 3.

THE DAY OF SORROW

October 14, 1876.

MY heart's desire is that the sweetness of Divine communion may to me be such that it will make all other wants forgotten.

October 15, 1882.

" This season has been sending me back to eighteen years ago, a never-to-be-forgotten time. I thought then that life could never again be lightsome, but I find that the more of Christ we enjoy the more we are able to bear."

October 15, 1886.

" I have learned in some measure that the Lord can fill the soul with Himself, where He takes away what seemed indispensable to our happiness."

October 14, 1888.

Himself with me has been quiet consolation in the day of sorrow.

" When we have truly found Christ, we can go through the world alone."

" In the world ye shall have tribulation, but draw the closer to Me ! "

" Never be offended at Christ's providences. He will recompense all to you, even in this life. '*A hundredfold more in this life.*' O believer, keep Him to His promise ! "

" When God has wiped away every tear from our eyes we shall see His providences very clearly."

" If you are a child of God there is nothing in the world you cannot do without, and have a heaven in the want of it."

" We are very apt to slight the Lord's discipline in small crosses, so He says, '*Despise not* the chastening of the Lord.' On the other hand, if the trial is very great we are apt to weary, and so He says, '*Faint not.*'"

" Jesus left His disciples in the little boat in the storm on the Lake of Galilee purposely that He might come to them in the fourth watch of the night and deliver them. I think He would have come to them sooner, perhaps in the first or second watch, if they had trusted Him."

" '*The joy of the Lord is your strength.*' Whatever is burdening you, get back to that joy of the Lord, and you are above the trouble. When harassed by a multitude of cares you have perhaps got from the Lord such a time of joy that for that time you were above all care. So in a time of affliction, when you retreat to the fortress, O how you will triumph! '*Though the fig-tree shall not blossom, neither fruit be in the vines.*' You walk out amid the desolation and look up—not around any more, and say, '*I will rejoice in the Lord, I will joy in the God of my salvation.*'"

"It is humbling to our self-righteousness to see that we have no reason whatever for anything but praise."

"They sung as it were a new song."

REV. xiv. 3.

THE GARMENT OF PRAISE

December 16, 1866.

THIS morning felt powerfully that if the Lord were to show us '*all His benefits*,' the sight would be too much for us to bear, for the contrast of our forgetfulness, ingratitude, selfishness, would rush upon us with awful power.

January 1, 1884.

I have been thinking of the Spirit bringing to remembrance past things. Lord, remind me of the mercies, the gifts, the blessings of the past year.

" Are you very thankful ? You know the difference between gladness and thankfulness. Gladness looks at the kindness and takes it all, but thankfulness looks at the Giver and loves Him for it all."

" Mercy is a stronger cord than suffering, far stronger than affliction."
" '*No man could learn that song*,' because

there is something in each one's experience that another cannot borrow."

"Earthly joy is a selfish thing, and so is earthly sorrow. Heavenly joy is the death of self."

"Christ had a delight in praise, possibly because it was a kind of echo from heaven. It reminded Him of the scenes He had left."

"The Church militant cries, Hosanna, the Church triumphant cries, Hallelujah."

"Christ known as Prophet revealing sin may give sorrow, but Christ as Priest puts on us the garment of praise and gives the harp."

"A gloomy believer is surely an anomaly in Christ's kingdom."

"Paul and Silas spread the Gospel over the whole city by their prayers and praises, and they thought it was to be by their preaching !"

"There is one ear that listens to every note of praise from every one of His people. God's heart is so quick and so tender that He can hear the hosanna of a little child. Never say, 'I need not praise Him. He will never miss me out of the choir.' 'Bless the Lord, O *my* soul.'"

"The Lord wishes us never to forget His past dealings. We should have a memory for them. In the kingdom we shall often-times remember the past. It will be a stream of joy to us to go back to the wilderness journey, the wilderness trials, and understand God's dealings with us, and how He led us by the pillar-cloud all the way. '*He that sitteth on the throne shall tabernacle among them,*' as if going over the desert scene again."

"'*God gave His only-begotten Son.*' He gave up the half of His own joy for a time for us."

" With the blood sprinkled upon
me, O may I get far up the hill
and meet God."

" Hitherto have ye asked
nothing in My name."

JOHN xvi. 24.

ASKING AND RECEIVING

WHEN I consider my time of late, our Lord's words ring in my ear, "*Have I been so long time with thee, and yet hast thou not known Me?*" I have not advanced in prayerfulness, nor have I grown to any great extent more than in former years. I live too much upon old manna.

October 6, 1877.

Have been able, amid much business, to get much of this day for prayer and meditation, having got preparation forward yesterday in great measure. Such a time is like climbing up the mount, and looking all around in calmness, seeing what our inheritance is, and thus better able to ask many things. O what a sense of poverty comes over me, looking at that wealth!

"What of the gold-diggings? Any recent discovery in the knowledge of Him who

126

counsels us to buy '*gold tried in the fire*'? Does not that mean such things as these?—

" ' Buy of Me your ransom-money.
  Buy of Me your golden harp.
  Buy of Me the golden streets of the New Jerusalem.
  Buy back Paradise, for the gold of that land is good.' "

"Let us be like Jacob's sons, go often to Joseph—our Joseph. The corn of the Nile that overflows yearly is the best, and is the likest to the corn of our God, proceeding as it does from His overflowing and everflowing love."

"Perhaps you would have grown in grace far more if you had used what God has given you for Him, and forgotten about yourself."

" 'It is more blessed,' said our Master, ' to give than to receive ' ; and then Paul and his friends prayed. Is not this as if he had said, 'Our Master delights to give, it is His blessedness to give. Come, then, let us kneel and ask Him for some gift.' "

"Let us put ourselves under the Holy Spirit's teaching anew, to be taught the Word, and how to preach the Word, not our thoughts upon it. One spark of lightning is worth a thousand of tame candle flames ; so one sentence given by the Holy Ghost is worth volumes of any other."

"Prayer will be very lame and dry if it does not come from reading the Scriptures."

"Workers cannot begin their work without a passage of Scripture for themselves. William Burns, when asked on one occasion to speak, said, 'No, I have not yet got a morsel for myself.' Try to act upon this principle, and remember it must be fresh manna, just gathered. I should feel ashamed to take withered flowers to the sick."

"Do you often try to meditate quietly? There are things God will show you in meditation that you will not find in the preaching of the Word, or in the assembly of believers.

> " 'There are crystals which cannot be formed
>   Till the vessel is cool and still.'

But remember that this leads to action. You must have got very little if you do not try to tell others of it."

"Meditation is letting God speak to us till our heart is throbbing."

"Enable me to live under the smile of Thy love, willing not to be noticed upon earth, if so I may glorify Thee more."

"Learn of Me; for I am meek and lowly in heart."

MATT. xi. 29

LOWLINESS OF HEART

September 9, 1848.

I THINK I see it to be somewhat as glorifying to God to keep our temper and happy frame of soul in the midst of common care, or in the midst of a rush of earthly vexations and annoyances, as it would be under the blast of persecution and dread of the sword and death. All the more glorifying, too, in the sight of God, because none else may be witness, and no motive of vainglory can creep in.

February 22, 1858.

The Lord has been teaching me to be willing to be least of all and servant of all. The soul of a weaned child is what I seek : meek and lowly in heart, with the eye upon the Lord alone. In this there is rest to the soul.

"It takes us all our days to learn these two things—to be meek and to be lowly."

"It is a test of our progress in sanctification that we are willing to have our faults pointed out to us, and that we don't get angry.

Why should we take offence at being told that we are not perfect?"

"God tells us to love reproof. I don't know any man who ever took reproof better than Eli. 'It is the Lord.' When Nathan said to David, 'Thou art the man,' he did not flare up as Herod did. No; he said, 'I have sinned,' and went away to write the fifty-first Psalm."

"There are some people who can stand anything but flattery. If no one ever praises you, you are all the better for it."

"It is a grace to give reproof rightly, and it is a grace to take it rightly. You may be sure you are safe in giving reproof if it costs you pain to do it. Rightly given reproof is sometimes a means of conversion."

"Are you willing to be a mote in the sunbeam, the beam of the Sun of righteousness?"

"It is natural for us to think if we could do some great exploit, or carry through some great piece of self-denial, we should be high in the kingdom. But it is not so. It is doing something that nobody sees but the Master Himself, and no one knows but He."

"Service for the Master that everybody praises is very dangerous service. Perhaps in the day the Master returns the name of one we never heard of in the Church of Christ may be the highest, because he did most, simply for the Master."

"We say, if we could but know something of what Christ did and said these thirty years in Nazareth! Why did He keep silence? To teach us the real nature of obedience. Is it not doing everything under His eye and for Him? He was teaching us not to mind the honour that cometh from man, to be content with the Father's approval. Do we seek to please the Lord thus, not asking 'What does man think,' but 'What does my Father in heaven think'? Is His approval enough for you, though all men should ignore you, or even despise you?"

" Lift our eyes heavenward. Earthward is bad enough, but inward is dreadful. Lift us heavenward to where Jesus sitteth on the right hand of God."

" Whither the Forerunner
is for us entered."

HEB. vi. 20.

THE UPWARD LOOK

April 13, 1867.

I SOMETIMES feel as if there were two sides to my soul, the one looking earthward, the other heavenward.

June 14, 1867.

My eye ought not now to look around for anything to stay me, but to look upward always for the glory there, and the Lord Himself who is to lead me in.

June 29, 1867.

I spent till midday fasting and praying. I sought as much to be drawn into His presence and to Himself as weaned from the world.

" After His resurrection Christ would be thinking of going home. It is the mark of every quickened soul that he feels his heart going upward."

" God's redeemed ones have got a beginning of heaven. They are independent of the earth."

THIRTY-FOURTH SUNDAY

" We have more to do with the world to come than with this world."

" The nearer you come to Him the better, for you will then be farther from the world, and the world will have least power over you."

" The world is so blind that it did not see the Light of the world when He came. How then can you expect that it will see His servants ? "

" The world is all that is outside of the soul's spiritual life."

" ' *God forbid that I should glory save in the Cross of our Lord Jesus Christ.*' The more I know of Him and His Cross, Paul says, the less I think of the world, and the less the world thinks of me."

" It is no easy matter to lay aside every weight, but when we look to Jesus the weights drop from our hand."

" We do not need new swords, new spears, new arms. We only need more eye-salve to see Who is on our side."

" When the Jews said that Stephen blasphemed Moses, the Lord put upon him the same glory that He put upon Moses, and his face shone."

" How often has God restored our soul ! How often has He fulfilled His promise that ' *they who wait upon the Lord shall renew their strength'!* and the world looked very small as we ascended on eagle's wings."

" This is heaven, to be with Christ. When a believer departs it is just as if he had gone up the transfiguration hill and gone to be with Jesus. The essence of heaven is Christ in the midst. Would it be heaven to you to be with Christ and to see Him as He is ? But you may have a daily visit to the transfiguration hill, and be getting daily a transfiguration blessing. Some of us say we got it at the Communion table, and we did not get it for months again. But any day we may climb the hill, and, if we want to be filled with joy unspeakable, *'hear Him.'*"

" As the bread is broken and the
wine is poured out, may we
feel that He is scarcely an
absent Saviour, though unseen."

" He was known of them
in breaking of bread."

LUKE xxiv. 35.

THE LORD'S TABLE

COMMUNION SABBATH, *June* 25, 1843.

A MOST blessed day. At the table, when giving thanks, I felt as if I could have stood there for ever to praise the Lord for His grace. I realised the blessedness of eternal praise in heaven.

January 28, 1877.

Our Communion. A time when my soul has learned a new lesson in regard to the helpfulness of trying to pray every hour of the day, though only for half a minute, and to praise in the same manner. To-day I was like a man standing in full sight of plenty at the door of a well-stored granary, all of it mine; but I took little of it.

> "One more day's work for Jesus,
> How sweet the work has been !
> To tell the story,
> To show His glory,
> When Christ's flock enter in.
> How it did shine
> In this poor heart of mine !'

THIRTY-FIFTH SUNDAY

April 10, 1881.

This Communion morning got some view of how deep may be the holy peace of a soul that sees the vastness of the Saviour's grace.

"I rode up to Blairgowrie to the Lord's Supper. I felt that there the Gift of God to sinners and the heart of God to sinners are so fully and exclusively set forth that the Lord's table is really the stereotyping of the Gospel."

"However weak you are, if you value supremely the atoning blood, come to the table."

"At the Communion table remember Him and forget yourself."

"There is nothing between a sinner and the Saviour, but there is something between the sinner and the Lord's table."

"Jesus is walking to-day among the seven golden candlesticks, and He will stop here at our Communion table, to see if any of us want anything from Him."

"Press the grapes of the promises into your cup, and drink of this wine of the kingdom. It will make you partaker of the Divine nature."

"Strong meat is not what are called the deep doctrines of Scripture. Strong meat is what we have at the Communion table, the finest of the wheat."

"If there is any time since the Fall that could be spoken of as heaven upon earth, it was that hour in the upper room when Jesus discoursed to His disciples. There could not be a wandering thought in that little company."

"Christ's nearer coming casts deeper solemnity over every Communion."

"Lord, give me for my hire some
lost pieces of silver."

" I have chosen you and
ordained you, that ye
should go and bring
forth fruit."

JOHN xv. 16.

May 29, 1871.

ANOTHER birthday. I have often this year wondered if my time for finishing my testimony may not now be near. I sometimes wish it were, and then I begin to think how in the future ages I shall be almost sorry that the days of trial, and serving God in the midst of it, are over ; the days of winning souls, sowing seed in tears. Lord, give me light, love, life, likeness to Thee.

June 21, 1884.

Lord, use me yet ! Lord, I love Thee and Thy work ; give me souls still before my sun has set, and give me more grace and knowledge of Christ. My light in daily life is very dim, I fear. But I shall see Christ glorified by the multitudes He has saved by others, and I shall rejoice in His joy."

" Did you ever feel in preaching as if you were a blunt arrow ? I felt so yesterday until about evening, when the Archer seemed to sharpen the point."

THIRTY-SIXTH SUNDAY

"' I have filled the bow with Ephraim' (Zech. ix. 13). When God uses you He just makes you an arrow—fills His bow with you."

"If God sends us to do anything for Him we have power, whether we know it or not."

"The Lord never asks us to go where He Himself is not going."

"' Take ye away the stone.' Christ likes us to do something, even though He is going to do greater things Himself."

"God always, or almost always, uses instruments to do His work. When His people are content to be saved themselves and not meddle with their neighbours, God will not meddle with them either. He will let them alone."

"Christ meets us in the path of duty. If the women had stayed at the sepulchre they would have missed the meeting with Chrst."i

"God can do anything by or for a man in Christ."

"God knows it is not good for His people to have easy work to do. He knows it is good for them to have hard work. When things are not to their taste, and when work is not pleasant, it is the best discipline for them. Jeremiah had almost made up his mind to go away back to Anathoth (Jer. xx. 14) and do no more public work. God does not say very much to him about it. He just sends him on another errand."

"I have come to believe this to be almost invariably true : that seldom is anything good proposed to us but we have something to object to in it at first. This seems to be the reason for the expression used by our Lord, '*Thrust forth labourers.*' We are all unwilling to go. The truth is, we are all a little lazy."

"The Lord never uses angels to preach the Gospel. It must be sinners that tell sinners what it is that takes away sin. God sends His people. 'You know every bush in which the sheep hide. Go you and seek for them.'"

" O for a heart like a glowing
coal, and an eye ever looking
full upon the Lamb!"

" Thy face, Lord, will I
seek."

PSALM xxvii. 8.

FOLLOWING FULLY

FELT for a time as if Jesus were very near, and I had such a view of Him as trustworthy and full of love that I felt I could ask, speak to Him, tell Him all I wished, and leave Him to care. More faith ! more faith !

"Let us stir one another up in the pursuit of holiness—fellowship with God. Samson's strength was only indicated by his long hair. It had a secret spring. Our success would not be our strength, nor would our enlarged preaching and diligent visiting, yet these will begin to grow if we have access to the hidden source."

"God will not use you for any special errand if you are not living daily near Him. A bright spark comes out of the furnace. Ah, but the furnace was well heated before."

"I am more than ever convinced that unholiness lies at the root of our little success. '*Holy men of God*' spake to the fathers.

146

It must be holy men still that speak with power."

"Rest in God is the oil for the wheels, and fellowship with one another is a help to the habit of rest. We must rest if we are to work, rest in God if we are to work for God."

"It is a rule in the Christian life that one grace exercised strengthens the other graces."

"We don't live upon experiences, but we ought to grow in experiences."

"Believers are not hired servants, supporting themselves by their own work, but children maintained at their Father's expense."

"Lot would not give up Christ, but he would not give up much for Christ."

"They are '*without fault before the throne of God.*' We don't wonder at that, for they are 'before the throne.' But here are believers on earth, and they are '*undefiled in the way!*'"

"In the temple there was an outer court. There were worshippers in that outer court, but the outer led into an inner, and those who were there were much nearer. Then there was a Holy of Holies, and those who got there were in the Lord's presence itself. I think I see in the disciples three stages. Yonder are the seventy He sends forth. Ah! but they are not so near as the twelve who are with Him wherever He goes. But of the twelve there are three who are nearer still. They go with Him to the transfiguration hill and see His glory, and they go with Him down to the garden. Yet of the favoured three there was one who lay on His bosom, the nearest of all. In the camp all the blood-sprinkled people got a blessing, but the seventy went up the hill and saw the God of Israel, higher than the rest. And Moses went highest up of all, to the pinnacle, and saw the glory."

" Blessed Saviour, Who art gone
to the mountain of myrrh and
hill of frankincense, impatient
in Thine own way till the day
break, fill us with the same
holy impatience."

Now is our salvation
nearer than when we
believed."

ROMANS xiii. 11.

THE COMING OF THE LORD

September 18, 1849.

THIS morning early I had awakened and looked out. It was about four o'clock. The morning star was shining directly before our window in a bright sky. One part of the window was misty with frost, the other clear, and through the clear part the star shone most beautifully. I thought of Christ's words, '*the bright and morning star*' (Rev. xxii. 16). Christ is all this to me in this world till the day break. I fell asleep, and when I next awoke the sun was shining through my room. Shall it not be thus at the resurrection? Our shadowy views of Christ are past, and now He is the Sun of righteousness.

"You will soon be a king. Why not think of your kingdom? Are you content with the Lord's gracious letter to you when you might rather be wearying for Himself? I know 'this same Jesus' is as precious to you as to any of us, but when will you be a 'man of Galilee,' gazing up into heaven?"

"We are to live for the Lord to-day, and look for His coming to-morrow."

"Some Christians make a great mistake. They think that because Christ said it was expedient that He should go away, therefore it is expedient that He should stay away. He went away to present His finished work to the Father, but He must come back again."

"'Work, for the night is coming,' says the hymn. But Paul says, 'The day is at hand; let us put on the armour of light.'"

"A people *prepared*, so that when the Lord comes He has nothing to do but take them up."

"Christ's coming draws nearer and nearer. '*When He cometh*' we may say in another sense than the woman of Samaria, and yet like her, '*He will tell us all things.*'"

"Moses' faith was such that he said, '*When they shall have come into the land.*' Even so do believers say now, '*When Christ, who is our life, shall appear.*' There is no doubt about it at all."

"Many people nowadays miss out the first part of the verse, '*the grace of God which bringeth salvation,*' and go on to talk of the next part, '*denying ungodliness and worldly lusts.*' You say, 'That's dreadful!' Yes, but I know some Christians who miss out the last clause altogether—'*looking for that blessed hope.*'"

"I find the thought of Christ's coming very helpful in keeping me awake. Those who are waiting for His appearing will get a special blessing. Perhaps they will get nearer to His Person. I sometimes hope it will be so, and that He will beckon me nearer to Him if I am waiting for Him."

" When we are forgetting Thee,
recall us to communion with
Thyself by some text, some
word of Thine own."

" He shall receive of Mine,
and shall show it unto
you."

JOHN xvi. 14.

July 31, 1890.

THERE is a simple spring of fresh water on the shore near our house here, over-flowing ; but, when the tide comes in, quite covered over. Still, the moment the tide recedes, there still is the ever-fresh spring. This is exactly what I find with myself. The influx of common things and various duties seems to lead my soul apart from the fellowship of the Lord ; but still the spring is there, and flows out again. But I grieve exceedingly at finding myself, when I awake at morning, like as if the tide had all night overwhelmed the spring, so that I have to seek for it and clear it out again. Oh, when shall this cease and the flow be un-interrupted ?

" Just a few days ago I had to ride after breakfast six miles off to visit, and scarcely got home in time to have ten minutes for dinner, when the hour of a teachers' meeting struck, and to this I had to go, and then from that to another. But that morning I had got this word, ' *The love of the Lord toward*

the children of Israel who look to other gods'
(Hosea iii. 1), and this grain of grace, this
particle of the fine wheat, this love to the
ungrateful, so continually recurred to my soul
that that day was a happy day amidst its
bustle."

"I think there might be written over
every Bible, '*With joy shall ye draw water out
of the wells of salvation.*'"

"Follow the Shepherd, and remember if
you are following Him you will be sure to
get a mouthful of pasture every now and
then. Our Shepherd would not lead us
where nothing is to be found."

"When we get a blessing from the Lord
part of it is to be given away. There is seed
for the sower, as well as bread for the eater."

"Many make pillows of God's greatest
truths, instead of girding them round them."

"'*Girt about with truth;*' that is, God's
revealed will. If you have only some pieces of
the truth your garment will hang quite loose."

"We need the Spirit of revelation to lead
us into all truth. When John was shown by
the angel the open gate of heaven he might
just have stopped there. But if he had, he
would never have seen the glories within.
We must do more than merely look at these
truths. We must go in and possess them."

"We are fed on the same food as those who have gone before us. They are on one side of the mountain in the sunshine, and we are on the other side in the shadow, but we are both getting the same pasture."

"God does not open the gates of the New Jerusalem and let the light fall on us in a flood. It would dazzle us into blindness. He gives us a little at a time, as we are able to bear it. When Moses wanted to see His glory He said, '*I will put My hand upon thee.*' He would not let him see all His glory, for it would have dimmed the eye of Moses before his time. So we must expect to get a little at a time, and just a little. Do not expect great revelations, and do not ask to be un-common Christians. Be content to be fed as all God's children are."

" Lord, before we put in the
sickle we ask Thee to whet it.'

"Not in the words which
man's wisdom teacheth."

I COR. ii. 13.

157

THE PREACHING OF THE CROSS

October 27, 1837.

I THINK that we are to be content to labour little comparatively, if we cannot water all with abundant prayers. Better do a little with prayer and in the Spirit.

December 20, 1862.

"Continued omission of the Gospel in our sermons, or passing from it quickly, arises from self-righteousness. We feel as if there was not so much need of pressing this truth. Whereas self-righteousness in minister and people is such that nothing but incessant repetition of the Gospel can be right."

"It is a remark of old and experienced men that very few men, and very few ministers, keep up to the end the edge that was on their spirit at the first."

"Preach Christ, for you cannot preach Christ without preaching sin."

"Christ is the lever by which God moves a world of souls."

"What God does in saving Gospel-hearers is to show them with power what they had previously known without power."

FORTIETH SUNDAY

" The blood of God-man is the mystery of godliness."

" The Cross was the breaking of God's alabaster box, the fragrance of which has filled heaven and earth."

" The Gospel is like the sun, it can look in at any window."

" It is a good thing angels were not sent to preach to us. I would go far to hear an angel preach, but I don't think I would get much good from his sermon. I would come away thinking of his beautiful words and his persuasive tongue, but perhaps saying, ' It is all very well for that angel to talk about the miry clay, but he does not know how stiff it is ; he never was in it ! ' "

" Knowledge of Christ is the preventive of backsliding. It fills the heart, and that keeps the world out."

" See that your last days are your best days —not like David, of some of whose descendants it was said in praise, ' they walked in the *first* ways of their father David.' "

" We are not to indulge for a moment in the belief, ' Oh, I must count on a season of languor in my Christian life.' Where did you find that in the Bible ?

> ' But like the palm-tree flourishing,
> Shall be the righteous one.'

159

Ask any gardener, and he will tell you it is a sad indication of any plant to stop growing."

"If you would really win the crown you must keep fast hold of the Cross."

"The safe side is Christ's side. He gets no wound in all His battles. He is conqueror in all He undertakes."

"'*Remember Jesus Christ*,' that He was of the seed of David, that He was raised from the dead, that this was Paul's Gospel (2 Tim. ii. 8)."

" There may be some one
troubled about how he is to
guide others, and guide himself,
through the wilderness. Make
him hear Thy voice saying,
' My presence shall go with
thee, and I will give thee
rest.' "

" They thirsted not when
He led them through the
deserts."

ISA. xlviii. 21.

THE WILDERNESS WAY

October 14, 1878.

THIS day fourteen years ago earth became to me a real wilderness, and I wondered how I could journey through it. But the Lord's presence and plenty of work for Him have borne me on.

April 17, 1887.

Many things have made earth to me more than ever a wilderness and a land of broken cisterns, but the Lord Jesus is more than ever a full heaven to me.

June 23, 1889.

The Lord is kinder to me than ever, the nearer I come to the end of my journey.

"None of God's pilgrims fall by the roadside."

"God will not give an easy journey to the promised land, but He will give a safe one."

"All who are under the shadow of the Paschal Lamb will be under the protection of the pillar-cloud."

FORTY-FIRST SUNDAY

"If God has a bottle for our tears and a book for our wanderings, I think He will also have a record of our joys and sorrows."

"The flaming sword turned every way to keep the way of the tree of life, but He who sheathed that sword now turns it every way to meet His people's wants."

"Those under the pillar-cloud feel its solemn shadow."

"Every part of a believer's reward sparkles with that name, 'My God.' That is what makes it so satisfying."

"'*The Lord is my Shepherd. I shall not want.*' Then you have everything but heaven."

"We every day escape dangers that we are not aware of. Is that not a beautiful touch in Jer. ii. 6, where God says He took care of Israel when they went through the wilderness —'a land of deserts *and of pits*'? They skirted the margin of these pits as the pillar-cloud led them safely along—a picture of how we are led. How we shall praise Him for all our deliverances!"

"When Israel reached the other side of the Red Sea, how surprised they must have been. No river like the Nile flowing through the land, no palm-trees heavy laden with dates, no gardens of cucumbers and melons! What was to become of them?

They were to learn that God could take
other ways and other means to lead them
onward. He took from them all visible
means of support, and then He stepped in
with the wondrous manna from the skies.
When the Lord takes away from His people
anything that they used to have, He does not
mean to make them unhappy. He wants to
make them happy in another way. He gives
them manna instead of bread. Corn is never
called ' *the bread of the mighty*,' but manna
is."

" Thou dost not take our excuses
for our poverty."

" There remaineth yet very
much land to be possessed."

JOSH. xiii. 1.

165

ANSWERED PRAYER

July 31, 1850.

I WISH I could pray for something new every day, while there are so many things in the treasury of God.

September 26, 1860.

It is my deepest regret that I pray so little. I should count the days, not by what I have of new instances of usefulness, but by the times I have been enabled to pray in faith and to take hold upon God.

January 1, 1890.

More carefully than ever I hope this year to give two hours before going out every day to meditation on the Word and prayer.

"The reason so many of the prayers of God's people bring down no answer is, they do not come from communion."

"Pray for blessing, for it is like the dew which Gideon prayed for. It falls where it is sought."

FORTY-SECOND SUNDAY

" There are a great many things God will not do till you put Him in mind."

" ' *That we may obtain mercy.*' Who can tell what saints get at the throne of grace, and what is wrapped up in that word 'mercy' ? "

" Christ never asked counsel of anybody except to bring out the thoughts of others, but did He ever fail to give counsel where it was asked of Him ? He did not need our help in His hours of distress, but we know how He runs to our help when we appeal to Him."

" When you begin to pray always get into this position, leaning on His bosom. Don't pray to some one far off. Don't pray even to some one in the same room."

" The blessing we pray for may not come at once, but it is on its way. Sometimes the Lord keeps us waiting long, because He likes to keep us in His presence."

" Sometimes in prayer we are vexed because we have forgotten something. But God allowed us to forget. He wanted us perhaps to attend to something else."

" Prayer for saints and for those who ' minister the Gospel ' is the oil which keeps bright all the weapons we use."

" ' *Ye ask and receive not.*' Perhaps you have not been careful to ask in the name of

the Lord. Or you have had a wrong motive.
It was for your own selfish advantage, not for
God's glory. What can it be if your prayers
are not answered? Can they all have been
'asked amiss'? What if the 'amiss' be here,
not expecting the answer? It came, and you
did not notice it. It may be lying there for
you, and you don't see it. If some great
requests are not answered it should solemnise
us, and make us look at our motive for
asking."

" We ask for conviction. We do not ask that it may be very deep, for we make idols of so many things that we might make an idol of our conviction. So we do not say anything about the depth, but we ask for the reality.'

" A broken and a contrite heart, O God, Thou wilt not despise."

PSALM li. 17.

THE SINFULNESS OF SIN

I GOT a very awful view of my long life's sinfulness in the evening. I seemed to myself to be one standing amid mercies of every kind, but specially Divine grace. The Spirit has been, since my conversion forty years ago, nearly continually putting to my lips full cups of blessing, and I have done little else than just take a few drops and then set the cup by! The Bible day by day; precious sermons; great books of truth; the lives of holy and happy saints; events of providence; all, all these, and my own preaching and the ordinances in which I take part; these, these have been each a full cup of blessing put to my lips; but scarcely ever have I done more than merely take a sip. Oh, what I have lost! Oh, what I have lost! My heart sinks within me. I can only once again put my hand upon the head of the slain Lamb, and look up. The words of Joel ii. 25 have been before now a comfort; for in some way the Lord will add that to all His other acts of grace. "*I will restore to you the years that the locusts have eaten.*"

FORTY-THIRD SUNDAY

May 4, 1883.

This morning awoke from a dream, in which I thought I got an amazing view of the greatness of one sin against such a God. How it made the atonement appear wonderfully great!

"Sin is not simply going against our conscience. It is going against the law, though conscience keep silence."

"When we count the pieces of the Ransom-money we see what a terrible evil sin is."

"God can pardon sin, but He cannot excuse it."

"God's grace is all against sin. The Gospel that brings a sinner to God exposes the sinner's sin and gives him the remedy, 'Go, and sin no more.'"

"If ever there was anything that, more terribly than hell itself, showed the sinfulness of sin, it was the Saviour's agony in the garden."

"I think Jesus will weep over the lost as He did over Jerusalem. It will be something to be said for ever in heaven, 'Jesus wept as He said, "Depart, ye cursed."' But then it was absolutely necessary to say it."

"I think that the shower of fire and brimstone was wet with the tears of God as it fell, for God hath no pleasure in the death of him that dieth."

"God is a sin-hater, but a soul-lover."
"No one ever honestly confesses before God the sin he has done, till that sin is taken away. It is a full pardon that makes a man guileless."

"The sinner has all the pride of a poor person who once was rich."

"Independence of God is bondage to Satan."

"Sorrow wells out of sin just as blood wells out of a wound."

"It is a real sense of sin that in a moment explains to us the richest figures in the Bible."

"Sorrow can never put away sin ; sacrifice alone can do that. So they not only wept at Bochim, but *they sacrificed there unto the Lord.*'"

"The Lord puts our 'folly' out of His sight as well as our sin, when He makes us 'the righteousness of God.'"

"A cloak of profession will make an awful blaze in that day when He burns the stubble."

"'*There is no man that sinneth not.*' This truth is the hypocrite's pillow, but the believer's bed of thorns."

172

" May we stand on the shore of
that ocean into which our sins
have been cast, and see them
sink to the depths, out of sight,
and the sea calm and peaceful
over them, the sunshine playing
on it, the sunshine of Thy love
and Thy favour."

" Unto you therefore which
believe He is precious."

1 PET. ii. 7.

THE ATONING BLOOD

September 28, 1879.

LET me record it to the praise of the glory of Divine grace and infinite mercy, that for many years, indeed as many as I can remember, since my first discovery of the sinner's way to God by Christ, I have never been allowed to lose my way to the mercy-seat for a single day. I have not always had bright sunshine, but I have every day had sunlight and not darkness in my soul. What shall I render to the Lord?

November 30, 1890.

The blood that takes away all guilt, the obedience that covers me with merit, O how precious!

"Christ needed the storm on the Lake of Galilee that He might show how His single word could quiet it. He needed a troubled conscience that He might show how His atoning blood could calm and quiet it. And He needed a great and guilty sinner in order to show the power of the atonement and the riches of His grace."

FORTY-FOURTH SUNDAY

" It is what we have seen and known of Christ that gives us communion, not what we have discovered of our own infirmities."

" There is nothing the devil is so much afraid of as the blood of Jesus Christ, God's Son."

" At the bush Moses was forbidden to draw nigh, but afterwards on the mount he went up into the very presence of God. What made the difference ? At the bush there was no sacrifice."

" By the seashore we are continually within sound of the ocean. Sometimes we hear the roar of its waves loudly and clearly, sometimes it is still and quiet. So the believer is continually within hearing of the voice of the atoning blood. Sometimes he hears it loudly and clearly, sometimes not so distinctly, but always there."

" ' That take for Me and thee '—all the Gospel is there, ' for Me and thee.' "

" In the joy of acceptance Isaiah cried, ' Lord, here am I, send me on any message.' If there is any duty you shrink from, come and lay your hand on the sacrifice, and you will get strength for it."

" Suppose that I, a sinner, be walking along yon golden street, passing by one angel after another. I can hear them say as I pass through their ranks, ' A sinner ! a crimson sinner ! ' Should my feet totter ? Should

my eye grow dim ? No ; I can say to them,
" Yes, a sinner, a crimson sinner, but a sinner
brought near by a forsaken Saviour, and now
a sinner who has boldness to enter into the
Holiest through the blood of Jesus."

" When I depart, let me be
remembered by Christ my
Priest, my Brother, my God."

" I turned to see the voice
that spake with me."

REV. i. 12.

THE KEYS OF DEATH

February 3, 1849.

REJOICED in the idea of it being *God alone* that I had to do with in going into eternity. He seemed so well known and sure. His heart is open. His grace has made all known to us.

March 10, 1866.

I see and believe that I should deal with Jesus just as did the twelve disciples, and should pray for my fellow-labourers, as if I were one of those praying for the seventy gone forth to the villages and towns. And then I may think of dying as just returning to tell Jesus all things that I have done and taught, and may expect to find Him as gracious, overlooking all defects, and rejoicing in spirit over even the little done in His name.

" The man who sees Christ in life is sure to see Him in the valley of the shadow of death."

" Christ has the keys of death, and it is He Who opens the gates and admits us into that invisible world. Then His will be the first face we see there—a known face."

"Dying is just more of Christ."

"What a happy thing it is that it is the kingdom of God our Saviour (2 Pet. i. 11). We know Him so well. It was He who put our robe of righteousness upon us (verse 1). We would be lonely in the great company if we did not know Him so well. Would it not be a great comfort to the dying thief that Christ said, 'To-day *with Me* in Paradise'?"

"Rest, glory, Christ. I think these three words tell all that we know of the intermediate state. The Holy Spirit always hastens us on to the resurrection."

"The intermediate state is heaven's upper room, where the Master is, and where He will say unutterable things."

"Paul was in the third heaven, Paradise, where '*the spirits of the just made perfect*' are gathered round the second Adam. There he heard unspeakable words. I think he must have heard the Saviour's voice speaking to His redeemed ones."

"Elijah would get a welcome when he went up, but what work he got we cannot tell. We do not know what work disembodied spirits get to do. Down here we are just at school and in the lowest class. But we shall have our grand work afterwards."

HEAVENLY SPRINGS

" Comparatively few of God's people have triumphant deaths. You are not triumphant when you fall asleep, and that is what death is, falling asleep. We should be living so that we could be ready to go any day. If you were to go to call upon some Christian friend, and the servant were to tell you at the door, 'Oh, he's gone!' would you feel you almost envy him? Are you living so that the only difference really that death would make would be to make you say, 'Well, my fellowship with the Lord will be closer, but I've had fellowship with Him all day'? When Elijah was told he was to be taken up, he went on doing his ordinary work, visiting the schools of the prophets. He did not spend the day in prayer or in any special preparation, as we call it. What we need for death is just what we need every day, the Saviour Himself with us."

" As we get into the enjoyment
of Thy love may we find that
we need scarcely any other
heaven, either here or here-
after, only more of this love,
and the continuance of it."

" There is none upon earth
that I desire beside Thee."

PSALM lxxiii. 25.

LOVE TO CHRIST

June 1, 1853.

FELT something of "*my soul longeth, yea, even fainteth,*" and I lie down this night intensely desiring to feel constrained by the love of Christ.

December 23, 1888.

I have been getting remarkable glimpses of Divine love in answer to earnest prayer that I might know "*the love that passeth knowledge.*"

"Pray often for me as poor and needy, with many of the stains of Sardis and Laodicea, and a flame as low as that of Ephesus on the altar of love to Him Who has so loved us."

"He that keepeth My commandments is he whom I love, not he that has a great glow of feeling toward Me."

"There are degrees of love. He will take the little, but He likes to have the much."

"If we had half the anxiety to know the

love of God that He has to make it known to us, we should never be in darkness."

"Let the love of Christ take possession of your heart, and you will find you are living for Him without an effort."

"'*In him, verily, is the love of God perfected.*' The love of God is blossoming out and bearing fruit in the man who keeps His commandments."

"We have but one thing to do, we have but one Person to please. Has your life been thus simplified?"

"John did not rise from the table because there was a doubt about himself and his steadfastness. He leaned all the harder on his Master's bosom."

"The prominent feature of the early disciples is they cannot leave Christ. They cling to Him, and if at any time, from fear or any other cause, they leave Him, we find them hastening back again. They kept His company, and were not of the world."

"Never drink at the cistern before going to the Fountain."

"Our heaven is up yonder with God. God's heaven is down here upon earth with us. His delights are with the sons of men."

"Christ's heart was left here when His body went up yonder."

"John was in the ship that night when

HEAVENLY SPRINGS

Jesus calmed the storm, and as the disciples
sailed with Him over a smooth sea they said
to one another, '*What manner of man is
this?*' Thinking of the great love of God
he says, '*What manner of love the Father hath
bestowed upon us!*'"

"Set Thy little children singing,
Lord, and then when Thou
hast set them singing Thou
wilt listen."

"He brought forth His
people with joy, His
chosen with gladness."
PSALM cv. 43.

JOY IN SORROW

March 21, 1847.

THERE is an intense joy in God which I have not yet drawn out of Him.

"Our time is shortening. The Master has been reminding me of this very solemnly, changing the blue sky over my head by the shade of lasting sorrow.

"But yet I know I shall Him praise."

December 29, 1884.

"I have lived seventy-four years in this world, and must be getting near the edge of the wilderness. But the prospect on before is very bright, the sadness is all in looking back. The more we know of Christ here the more of heaven we enjoy."

"Jacob said, 'I shall go down to the grave with sorrow.' What a mistake! He went down singing!"

"Those who sing loudest in the kingdom will be those who on earth had the greatest bodily suffering. We pity them now, but then we shall almost envy them."

FORTY-SEVENTH SUNDAY

"We are like children trying the strings of the harp which we expect yet to use."

"The sweetest songs are those which go up to God from a bereaved heart from which He has taken its most loved object."

"'*All joy and peace in believing.*' All joy, complete joy, that will fill every crevice of your vacant heart. All peace, that will not allow room for a single fear."

"Paul is like a man climbing a mountain, sometimes on an eminence and in the bright sunshine, sometimes down in a shady hollow, sometimes wrapped in mist and gloom, but always singing!"

"It is not only at first that believers sing. Their songs are sweeter still as they get nearer the kingdom, and they expect soon to get the golden harps. I can't tell what notes may be brought out of these harps when a sinner's fingers touch the strings."

"When present affliction strips us of all earthly comforts, so that we can adopt Habbakuk's words; if it makes us look within the veil and hear Christ saying, 'Am I not better than all My gifts?' then affliction is a blessing. How far will the blessing go? It worketh out for us an eternal weight of glory. Affliction for a moment, then an eternity of glory to recompense it! Instead of there being just a possibility that the affliction may do you good, Paul says 'It is beyond measure efficacious. You could not do without it.' To Paul the heaviest affliction seemed but a feather resting on his soul, because he lived so much within the veil. If we cannot, like him, say 'Our light affliction,' let us try to say at any rate, 'It is but for a moment.'"

" Lord, fill me with the Holy
Ghost and the mind of Christ."

" Who went about doing
good."

ACTS x. 38.

BROTHERLY LOVE

August 24, 1835.

I FEEL this a consolation, that if I have done no other good, I may have given "a cup of cold water" to some disciple yesterday, and that shall not lose its reward in heaven.

May 19, 1866.

Have been learning from Christ's stay on the earth during forty days after His resurrection, all for the sake of others, that disciples ought not to be too eager for glory, but should, for the sake of others, their families, their friends, the world, desire to continue here a while.

June 17, 1839.

"Remember me to the saints among you. If ever they got one cup of cold water from me to their souls, I have a claim on their prayers."

"God loves His saints so much that He will give a reward to any one who gives one of them a cup of cold water."

FORTY-EIGHTH SUNDAY

" A believer is not very holy if he is not very kind."

" Paul says that even for the sake of comforting the saints he would wish to abide in the flesh."

" I think it is a very poor kind of holiness that does not make us care for others."

" To keep a believer's lamp bright is one of the highest benefits you can confer on a dark world."

" How much we may be to blame for the faults of others not being cured ! We point to their faults and failings, but we don't pray for them."

" ' *I, after I heard of your faith in the Lord Jesus, and love unto all the saints, cease not to give thanks for you, making mention of you in my prayers.*' We should have said, ' There is no need to pray for them now ; they are all right.' When Paul heard of their faith and love he just prayed for them the more."

" In the parable of the pounds each man got one pound. One made his pound ten, and Christ said, ' Well done.' Another made it only five, but Christ did not scold him. He said, ' Well done.' I think we should act on the same principle."

" Faith does a great deal for us. It unites us to Christ. Hope does a great deal for us.

191

How it brightens the future ! But love flows out of ourselves to others."

"'Little children' is the name for the family of God in every place and at every time. John learned the name from Christ at the first Communion-table. Christ only said it once, and John, leaning on His bosom, caught it up and repeated it."

"Brotherly kindness is confined to the household of faith. Love has no limits but the world."

"Give us a taste of the grapes
of Eshcol that we may long
for the promised land."

"The things which God
hath prepared for them
that love Him."

1 COR. ii. 9.

THE BELIEVER'S INHERITANCE

April 26, 1864.

TO-DAY Isaiah lvi. has been very sweet. It stills all earthly ambition. "*A name better than of sons and daughters*," the Lord's own favour.

December 3, 1867.

To-day I thought I got new insight into the words, "*Ask and ye shall receive, that your joy may be full.*" As if the Lord had said to them, "Now, make it your rule to ask as much, and to ask the very things that will make your joy full." Always ask till you get your cup running over.

July 13, 1873.

"*He that overcometh shall inherit all things.*" I cannot take in the beauty and the suggestions of peace and joy that arise ; my heart just yearns for some inexpressible joy. But I shall inherit "all" yet.

"If the Lord has done much for you, that is a reason for expecting more. If He has taken you into Jairus' house to see the resurrection, He will take you up the mount to see the transfiguration. Instead of folding your hands and saying, 'He has filled my cup,' ask Him to fill it over again."

"Let us not carry away a little from the Lord and say to any one who asks us, 'This is what we got from the Master, these one or two grapes.' But let us take the great cluster of Eshcol grapes and say, 'This is our Master's manner of giving.'"

"Listen to Paul's words, 'Who is he that condemneth? Look at the robe I have got by going for it! Nay, I am more than conqueror through Him that loved me!' He is waving his palm as well as wearing his white robe. Can you say this? You say, 'I contrive to keep the enemy back.' But you should be '*more than conquerors.*'"

"God no sooner said to Moses, 'My presence shall go with thee,' than Moses hastened to ask something more, '*I beseech Thee, show me Thy glory.*'"

"We know what the blessedness of pardon is, but we have yet to know the blessedness of not needing a pardon any more. We have 'strong consolation' now under any trial, but what shall it be when we shall never have a sorrow to need consolation? He wipes away our tears now, but what will it be not to

have a tear to wipe away? We are just in
the dawn of the daylight."

"There is a joy in reserve for us such as
cannot be described, that will make us say of
the 'joy unspeakable,' 'a beginning!'"

"We go forward, praising Thee
for all past mercies, and trusting
Thee for every step of the
way."

"Not one thing hath
failed of all the good
things which the Lord
your God spake concern-
ing you."

JOSH. xxiii. 14.

THE GIFT OF GOD

August 26, 1880.

IT is wonderful that now for fifty years the Lord has kept me within sight of the Cross.

May 29, 1889.

The Lord has enabled me to lean upon Christ day by day for nearly sixty years. He took hold of me and has never once left me in darkness as to my interest in Him, all that time. I have been meditating upon His marvellous grace and I see it in this light. He promised that day I found Him that I would have rest in Himself always as I went along, and then nothing less than a whole eternity of blessedness. All this for accepting the Gift of Christ! The first moment of faith rewarded by everlasting ages of blessedness!

"If you take the pardon, the Hand that gives it to you will be clasped in yours to bring you into fellowship with Himself."

"Why is believing so important? It empties us of self. All the glory must be given to God."

FIFTIETH SUNDAY

"If any of you ask, what is great faith? The reply is, having a great opinion of Christ."

"Great faith is simple faith. If you are seeking great faith, remember, the simpler it is, the greater it will be."

"Believers are great unbelievers. They are slow to believe *all*."

"Very much of unbelief consists in believing half of what God tells us, and not the whole."

"Our unwillingness is our inability."

"Unbelief is never at a loss for an excuse, and an excuse is just a lie."

"There is such a thing as leaving our first faith, as well as our first love."

"Faith keeps us, but God keeps our faith."

"If you say it is good to have doubts, you are just saying it is not good to take all that God offers."

"There were many who touched Christ in the press, but only one who touched Him drew virtue out of Him."

"Learn to read your title to the family of God by what God has said, not by a special message to yourself."

"'My' is the handle of faith."

"It is not said he who 'feeleth' is passed from death unto life. It is he who 'believeth.' It is not he who 'loveth,' but he who 'believeth'; not he who 'prayeth,' but he who 'believeth.' We stand at Calvary and hear Christ say, 'It is finished.' We say 'Amen,' and put the cup of life to our lips."

"Shepherd of souls, hide me in
Thy faithfulness."

"That I might finish my
course with joy."

ACTS xx. 24.

IN OLD AGE

December 2, 1888.

I HAVE been thinking to-night that perhaps my next great undertaking may be this, "*appearing at the Judgment-seat of Christ*," when I give an account of my trading with my talents. I wish to hide in the shadow of the Plant of Renown, and be found there when the voice says, "Where art thou?"

September 25, 1891.

Yesterday and to-day I have had some glimpses within the veil, as if to prepare me more for what may now soon come. It is very solemn to find myself near the threshold of eternity, my ministry nearly done, and my long life coming to its close. Never was Christ to me more precious than He is now.

" 'Why am I spared so long in health?' is a question I often ask. One thing I know, it must be that I may preach and commend Christ and Him crucified wherever and whenever it is in my power."

FIFTY-FIRST SUNDAY

"Lengthened life should be lengthened work."

"Our root is in Christ and in the love that passeth knowledge. We will 'grow up and flourish' if our roots are in such a soil. If spared to old age our fruit will be abundant. In our younger days a great deal was blossom, but as we grow older it is fruit. It does not make such an appearance, but it is more enduring."

"Life and godliness—the sap of the tree and the fruit."

"A man may be lost by doing nothing. He may be among the wicked by not trading with his talent."

"Ours is constant work, but it is vineyard work, and work for the Master who bore the burden and heat of the day."

"Let us give thanks for life and work, even for care and weariness."

"'Come, ye blessed of My Father.' That word 'come'—how it will sound through our heart! It was the word that drew us first to Him, and it will draw us into the kingdom."

"'Lord, now lettest Thou Thy servant depart in peace.' Thou art dismissing me from my post. It is the same word used where Christ 'sent away' the multitude at evening. 'Lord, Thou art sending me home in peace at evening.'"

" I sometimes think it was God's way of keeping Joshua humble that He said to him after he had subdued the thirty-and-one kings, and perhaps was taking a rest, ' *Joshua, thou art old and stricken in years, and there remaineth yet very much land to be possessed.*' "

" The night cometh, but thereafter the morning, the resurrection-morning, when we shall know the results of present labour, and when we shall see Him as He is. It is a solemn thing to look back on so many years as I have had, and to look a little onward and see the eternal shore."

" Oh the memories of the past ! It needs the Man that is the Hiding-place to keep them."

" We may have a rough part of the wilderness still to travel, not like those who are around the throne, but it is just one day at a time, and one Sabbath at a time."

" They came to Elim."

EXOD. xv. 27.

THE LAND OF PROMISE

May 28, 1892.

IF spared till to-morrow I shall have finished the eighty-second year of my pilgrimage. When I read the other day that verse in Deut. ii. 7, "*The Lord thy God hath blessed thee in all the works of thy hand; these forty years He hath been with thee, thou hast lacked nothing,*" I said to myself, "These eighty-and-two years He has been with me," twice the time mentioned there, and I can truly say "I have lacked nothing." More than that, He has given me "*that blessed hope,*" the prospect of being for ever in the kingdom with Him who has redeemed me by His blood. It was in the year 1830 that I found the Saviour, or rather that He found me, and laid me on His shoulders rejoicing, and I have never parted company with Him all these sixty-two years.

"We were reading this morning, Joshua v. ; the manna ceased only when they really had crossed the Jordan, and as for the cloudy pillar no notice is taken of its ceasing excepting this. The Lord says : 'As Captain of the host am I *now* come.' It was as much as saying : 'I have hitherto led you through the wilderness in the cloud, but now the end of that is come, and so I appear as Captain of the host, leading you all into the land.' Some day it shall be thus with us. We shall suddenly find Bibles, and ordinances, and living by faith (our manna) all ceasing, for sight has come and the realities of the unseen glory, and we shall find our God and Guide suddenly present to us in the Person of the Saviour, 'Whom not having seen we loved.' "

" If the Father has the kingdom ready for us He will take care of us on the way."

" When your foot swells the Lord does not want you to travel."

" Never be perplexed as to the next step ; that is the Lord's work."

" When new troubles come, God has new ways of bringing us out of them."

" Jesus never says, '*Make* thy cross,' but '*Take* thy cross and follow Me.' "

" The safeguard of God's little ones is to look at Him who keeps them."

" There might be in the history of each of God's people a book of Deuteronomy, going over again the wilderness journey."

HEAVENLY SPRINGS

" Pilgrims have always been pilgrims, and
the desert has always been the desert, but
Christ is always Christ, the same ' yesterday,'
when John lay on His bosom, and ' to-day '
when you and I may do the same, and ' for
ever,' when at His coming we shall know
and feel all the bliss of being one with Him."

" O that I and the children Thou
hast given me may be with
Thee in the kingdom, walking
together in the streets of the
New Jerusalem, each adding
another note to the heavenly
song ! "

" Our gathering together
unto Him."

2 THESS. ii. 1.

FOREVER WITH THE LORD

January 1, 1865

HOW solemn the review of both the past and the future ! Lord, may I follow the ark, and may my children all do the same, as did the little ones of Israel when passing the river.

August 24, 1867.

Our times are very threatening times. I sometimes fear for my children, only I see the Lord who kept Noah kept his children also, when a whole world rebelled.

August 6, 1885.

For several days I have had time and freedom in the forenoon to spend two hours in prayer. To-day, when thus engaged, I was led forward in thought to realise myself standing before the Lamb, without a single sinful tendency, and without one drawback in the way of the slightest uncertainty. " *For ever with the Lord.*" For ever with all those holy, happy friends. For ever, for ever, holy and without blame, like the Lamb Himself !

FIFTY-THIRD SUNDAY

" My righteousness is the righteousness of Him who is God and our Saviour. I see nothing in myself but what would condemn me to eternal banishment from God. I shall be to all eternity a debtor to the Lord my God, never paying one mite, but, on the contrary, hour by hour getting deeper and deeper and deeper in debt to Him who is " *all my salvation and all my desire.*" I often exult in the thought that every moment in the ages to come I shall be better and better able to love Him Who loved me from all eternity—Who chose me—Who lived for me that life of obedience, and died that death in order that I, a soul that sinned, might live with Him for ever. He rose, ascended, interceded for me. He presented my name to the Father as one of the lost whom He had found. He is coming in glory soon to claim my body from the grave, and to make me altogether perfect, spotless, glorious, the image of Himself. All to the praise of the glory of His grace ! All this is mine because He has enabled me to believe on the beloved Son. " *Accepted in the Beloved*" shall be on my forehead along with the Father's name, in New Jerusalem. *By grace, through faith* ' *Bless the Lord, O my soul !* ' "